Praise for *Simply an Inspired Life*

"If you are looking for a kind, gentle, and nurturing guide to personal growth, *Simply an Inspired Life* is the book you need. Mary Anne Radmacher and Jonathan Lockwood Huie carefully guide you through the important aspects encountered on any spiritual path, focusing on the key elements that will lead you to greater peace and inner happiness. Using true-to-life examples and simple but potent exercises, these two experts will have you letting down your resistance and opening your heart and mind to expansive changes. What a blessing!"

—**DR. SHERI A. ROSENTHAL**, author of *The Complete Idiot's Guide to Toltec Wisdom* and *Banish Mind Spam!*

"As an artist, I am painfully aware that creativity is impossible without that most elusive quality—inspiration. The truth is that inspiration has to be rooted in an inspired life! I would highly recommend Mary Anne Radmacher and Jonathan Lockwood Huie's *Simply an Inspired Life*. They've written a practical and powerful guide that will direct you along a visionary pathway to your most creative life."

—**SUSAN BOURDET**, artist

"If you want to know how to use your life as your path to joy and fulfillment, then *Simply an Inspired Life* is for you. Radmacher and Huie show how to take the ups and downs of life and use them as the method for getting a life of deep fulfillment. Highly recommended."

—**DMITRI BILGERE**, co-founder of Shadow Work Seminars and author of *Beyond the Blame Game*

"Unlike many self-help books, the words of these fine authors remind us of our own power to change our lives without the residue of inadequacy that a book of 'how to' sometimes leaves behind. There's nothing but smooth SAILing in *Simply an Inspired Life*. Well done!"

—**JANE KIRKPATRICK**, award-winning author of *A Flickering Light* and *A Simple Gift of Comfort*

Simply *an* Inspired Life

Consciously Choosing Unbounded Happiness in Good Times & Bad

Accept your past, release your expectations
& recognize your choices!

Mary Anne Radmacher
Jonathan Lockwood Huie

Conari Press

First published in 2009 by
Red Wheel/Weiser, LLC
With offices at:
500 Third Street, Suite 230
San Francisco, CA 94107
www.redwheelweiser.com

ISBN: 978-1-57324-457-2
Library of Congress Cataloging-in-Publication Data is available upon request.

Cover design by Donna Linden
Text design by Maxine Ressler
Typeset in Adobe Garamond, Charlotte Sans, and Futura
Cover image © Selin Ogeturk/iStockphoto.com

Printed in Canada
10 9 8 7 6 5 4 3 2 1
The paper used in this publication meets the minimum requirements of the American National
Standard for Information Sciences-Permanence of Paper for Printed Library Materials Z39.48-
1992 (R1997).

Table of Contents

Simply *an* Inspired Life

Introduction

I'm not afraid of storms, for I'm learning how to sail my ship.

—Louisa May Alcott

For yesterday I hold no apologies.
For tomorrow I offer no answers.

—mary anne radmacher

Life is a journey—enjoy it.

—jonathan lockwood huie

MAR Choose joy. There is always a choice, and a grand choice is joy. There. If you must hurry about your day—you now know the core premise of this work.

I call this "work" because it *is* work. Choosing joy requires evaluation, observation, and willingness to travel from where you are right now. As I considered starting my creative business, I assessed, "The jump is so frightening between where I am and where I want to be. Because of all I may become, I will close my eyes and leap."

This work is about that. It's the work of becoming the finest, most joyful version of yourself—making the jump to joy. It is an opportunity to take the leap, not just with your eyes closed, but rather fully open and wide awake.

JLH In this journey from suffering to joy, quick-fix solutions won't work. Neither will just saying, "Put on a happy face," and pretending that everything is OK. Please accept our challenge to your fundamental ways of thinking and seeing, as we suggest ways you can change lifelong habits of suffering and ultimately invite joy into your every day.

Some people get stressed by the smallest provocation, while others retain joy and serenity even in the face of life's most severe challenges. Part of the difference is genetics, part is environment. Regardless, each of us can be in charge of our emotions—not by biting our lip and struggling on, but by training ourselves to react differently to the stresses of life.

The consequences of the events and emotions of the past are often painfully apparent today. We will guide you in revisiting your past in order to strip old emotions away from underlying events. You can *choose* to change your interpretation of what happened. Honor your past not by continuing to suffer in its memory, but by re-clothing its naked facts in bold and empowering new stories and emotions.

Assumption and expectation trigger suffering. When life doesn't occur as we expect that it *should*, we suffer disappointment. You are probably not aware of all the assumptions and expectations you actually have of life, so our task will be to illuminate them and then to question them.

Our memories of past events—even the recent past—seldom match what a video camera would have recorded. Rather than being only an issue of faulty memory, this is mostly an issue of perception. Even in the present, we don't see the same scene as a video camera. Usually, we see what we *assume* is happening, or what we have prepared ourselves to see. For example, if thirty-five children are posing for their school yearbook group photo, the camera records each one with equal precision. As you stand next to the photographer, you see your own daughter with great clarity—you'll remember this moment forever. But you're likely to be essentially oblivious to the children you do not know, and will remember nothing of how they looked. In this book, we will practice awareness and will *choose* the perspective from which we perceive our world. This will transform *what* we see by changing *how* we see.

WHAT DOES AN INSPIRED LIFE LOOK LIKE?

You are living an Inspired Life when you are consistently joyful, compassionate, loving, and thankful to be exactly who you are, regardless of external events and circumstances. You no longer suffer from blame, disappointment, and worry. You appreciate the distinction between *events* and your *feelings* about those events, and you are consistently able to choose a joyful interpretation of events.

If I'm living an Inspired Life, can I still break a leg? Unfortunately, yes. An Inspired Life is about choosing your response to physical events rather than about changing those events. Stress-related ills will likely improve significantly, but the broken leg . . . sorry.

Take wing and soar to gain the broad view.
—jlh

Have you heard the ancient story of the blind men and the elephant? One man touched the elephant's leg and concluded that the leg *was* the elephant. One touched the trunk and concluded that the trunk was the elephant. One touched the tail, and concluded that the tail was the elephant. Others touched other parts, and each concluded that the part he touched was the elephant.

Each blind man touched the part of the elephant that was nearest to him and assumed that he had learned the nature of the elephant.

Like the blind men, we touch some part of life and *assume* it to be the entire nature of life. We look at life from the perspective of our heritage, our community, and our experience, and we assume that we fully appreciate all of life.

"What We Know," "What We Know That We Don't Know," and "What We Don't Know That We Don't Know."
—Werner Erhard, describing the three ways we relate to knowledge

We invite you to challenge your perspectives and your belief systems—whatever they are. Together, we will create a little crack in your assumptions and expectations of life, allowing light to shine through.

Our Voices

Simply an Inspired Life (SAIL) has two authors. Mary Anne and I (Jonathan) do not speak with a single voice. We are individuals—each with our own story to tell. This book is the product of interweaving our unique styles and different points of view on the subject of what it means to live Simply an Inspired Life.

To distinguish our writing typographically:

MAR   Mary Anne's writing looks like this.

JLH   Jonathan's writing looks like this.

Others' quotes look like this.

ABOUT THIS BOOK

MAR   This material is presented in a purposely designed sequence, most effectively read from beginning to end. Alternately, you might browse the table of contents for chapter titles or subheadings that call to you on a particular day.

There are a number of written exercises in this book. The process by which you record your thoughts is less significant than doing the actual exercises in the manner you are most at ease. Writing with pen and paper connects me more deeply to my experience. It is a slower and more methodical process than using a keyboard. Some people are more at ease with verbalizing their thoughts using a handheld recording device. Pursue the process that inspires you to move forward with the exercises.

JLH *Simply an Inspired Life* is designed to make you feel better about yourself, but also to challenge you. Whenever you feel uncomfortable with what you are reading, reflect by writing about your discomfort. Exactly which ideas are causing discomfort? What are your body sensations? What is the conflict with the ideas you brought to this book? Is there another time in your life that brought up similar feelings? Consider looking at the world from a different point of view just for the few minutes it takes to read a chapter. What might be gained from looking at the world from a different perspective? The journey to an Inspired Life requires different things from each of us. Common to us all is the courage to simply begin.

Chapter 1
Simply an Inspired Life

We cannot direct the wind, but we can adjust the sails.
—attributed to Bertha Calloway
(Founder of the Great Plains Black Museum)

capture a shadow,
dance with the wind,
stand in a rainbow,
begin at the end.

—mar

Play with life, laugh with life, dance lightly with life, and
smile at the riddles of life, knowing that life's only true
lessons are writ small in the margin.

—jlh

JLH   Remember the story of the blind men and the elephant from the introduction? That is how we will approach our discovery of Simply an Inspired Life—walk around it, touch the trunk, the legs, the tusks, the tail, and yes, we're going to have to examine the scat—that's part of life also. It is important to appreciate all of life.

In mastering the art of living Simply an Inspired Life—increasing your joy and decreasing your suffering—you will become more and more skilled at distinguishing between what happens and how you feel about what happens—the distinction between *events* and your *feelings* about those events.

BECOME A PASSIONATE OBSERVER OF LIFE

To gain consistent access to joy and serenity, you will break some lifelong habits—habits so ingrained, so much a part of you, that they have become invisible, like water to a fish.

The secret to overcoming these limiting habits is observing other people in action. Through detachment and conscious attention, you can identify well-defined patterns of emotionally self-destructive behavior that ravage peace and happiness.

After recognizing these patterns in others, you can hold a mirror to yourself and consider accepting that you share these same self-destructive behaviors.

Begin your observations by watching and listening to those you don't know well. Life experiences always color our perceptions with preformed judgments, but because we don't have an emotional investment in strangers, we come as close as possible to being objective.

A busy coffeehouse is a microcosm of the world and an ideal place to begin observing. Give it a try. When observation exercises are suggested, consider doing them in a coffeehouse where you can anonymously study people.

Hold a Mirror to Yourself

MAR I was stuck in a consistently negative phase. My new business was difficult. My health was wavering. A significant partner was unsatisfied with many of my qualities and habits. Friends were concerned that I'd sacrificed my security for this business based entirely on my creative writing. Community members found fault in the ways I conducted my commerce and public service.

In a moment of discouragement, I realized I had to turn this experience around.

Instead of repeating and focusing on the negative assessments, I wrote down the exact opposite. I noted the swing side of the critical statements. I also recorded the opposite of harsh commentary I'd delivered to myself. This was an everyday process for a full month. As each day progressed, I would return to day one of the project and read from start to finish. By the end of the thirty days it took quite a bit of time to read all that had been written.

My, oh my. What an amazing person I discovered I was while reading those pages of positive assessments. There it was in writing—I was beautiful, stylish, and just the ideal size. I was savvy, a good planner, and I had the required tools to operate my small business. That was just the start. After thirty days of this—the process disclosed many things to me that I had not previously seen.

A significant uncovering was that so much of the negative talk from others was really a reflection of their attitudes toward themselves. And my own negative assessments arose from fear of failure more than from an accurate evaluation of my abilities and ways. This process lifted me to a different level of telling stories, one where I could turn projection into positive purpose and tell stories which featured me, in all my finest qualities, as the capable hero. The creative writing process has been helpful through the whole of my life when I've needed a mechanism for changing negative patterns. It can be extremely helpful, even if only practiced for a single day.

Projection

JLH We only see what we are looking for. This is especially true as we observe our friends and family—we only see in them what we are ready to see. And what is that? We are prepared to see our own qualities showing up in others.

If we are happy, we are prepared to see others looking and sounding happy. But if we are sad, we are prepared to see sadness. If someone says, "Lovely day, isn't it?" our reaction is somewhat influenced by their tone of voice, but is even more swayed by our own emotional state. We may hear joy in every fiber of their being, or we may hear empty filler or even sarcasm.

Projection is regrettably common in romantic relationships. For instance: I have come home from a hard day at work, I'm grouchy, and my spouse and I start bickering. I say angrily, "Why do you always have to get upset with me?" What is going on? Projection. I am the one who is angry, but I see my spouse as the angry one. I see my own anger in the mirror of my spouse, but I believe that the anger is "out there," removed from me.

Projection originates from our past too. It can cause us to see our partner as a person who is likely to leave the relationship, to have an affair, to mismanage money, not to pull his or her own weight, to get lazy or fat, or not to be a good parent. At least

partially, and sometimes solely, this is because a previous partner or lover had demonstrated those qualities. We also project
onto our partner those qualities that we observed our parents
exhibiting toward each other.

Early in our relationship, my wife, Suze, and I developed a
caution-flag phrase to remind each other when we see this happening: *Don't project your past onto my future.* Caution phrases
can be a powerful shortcut to nipping a contentious moment,
but only if both partners have agreed on the signal.

TODAY IN MY WORLD:

Today, find a place to observe strangers talking—possibly a busy
coffeehouse. Pay attention to the conversations around you, and
listen for projection. How do you feel when you hear it?

The Stories We Tell Ourselves

Other than physical pain—such as a toothache—all our suffering is emotional suffering. The majority of the suffering we experience in life is not caused directly by events and circumstances,
but by our emotional responses—which we have the ability to
alter.

Consider this common situation: I make a lunch appointment
with a friend—call her Jane. I am careful to be at the agreed-
upon place at the agreed-upon time, but Jane never comes—no
phone call, nothing. It's not fair. She wasted my time. She disre-
spected me. The tangible damages from the event are relatively
small—the gas and parking money, the time I could have used
otherwise, the conversation I didn't have. But the self-inflicted
emotional suffering may border on devastating.

I had an expectation that my friend would be there, and I suffered disappointment when she wasn't. My friend should have

been there. She was wrong not to be there. It's her fault—she is to blame. I also have a nagging fear that Jane has suffered an accident, and a fear that she no longer likes me.

A video recording of the event would show no assault having occurred, but to me the emotional suffering hurts as much as a dagger thrust into my heart. With the perspective of Simply an Inspired Life, though, I can see that the suffering is self-inflicted and can be replaced with a happier emotion.

For everything I experience or observe, I create a story—not sometimes, but always.

—jlh

As I am sitting alone at that table set for two, my mind is chattering away. I am creating a story about how my friend is terribly inconsiderate and life is so unfair.

In this book, we define *story* as something we tell ourselves about what has happened or is happening. The stories we tell ourselves are always different from what a video camera would record. Our story may add to the facts—as in the example above—or it may omit crucial facts, or change facts—either just a little or completely.

Understanding Our Stories

Why do we create stories? Creating stories is not our choice—it's instinctive—and we usually have no idea that we are such creative storytellers. If you doubt that you are a constant and creative storyteller, consider another lunchtime situation.

I have lunch with two friends. Later I find the two arguing about what was said during the lunch. Moreover, I find myself surprised that neither of their recollections of the conversation matches my own.

My friends are not lying, crazy, or suffering from Alzheimer's. Each has simply created a unique story to describe the lunch. While their stories are partly based on the events that a camera would have recorded, they are also influenced by each person's history, expectations, emotional state, and much more. My own recollection of that conversation wouldn't match a recording of the lunch either, and it is also a story.

Trying On Happier Stories

Being a natural-born storyteller is not bad or wrong—it is just what human beings are, all the time. Our path to freedom from suffering lies in the recognition of our storytelling nature. Accepting that we are constant storytellers provides us with the opportunity to understand our stories and then to change them.

We do not need to be at the mercy of an unconscious voice somewhere in the back of our mind feeding us painful stories. We have the power to consciously create alternative explanations for what we see and hear. We can try on other explanations—stories—to create a more favorable view of our experiences.

Whenever my story portrays me as a victim, I can reasonably infer that the person I am painting as a callous villain has his own very different story to tell. Perhaps it wouldn't be a very believable or sympathetic story, but it might be an even better explanation for the situation than my own story. Remember that neither party's story matches what a video camera would have recorded—and perhaps neither story even resembles the video recording.

Look again at that disappointing lunch appointment when my friend stood me up. Jane almost certainly has a different story about that event—a story in which she is not a villain and perhaps is the victim. She may have been waiting at another restaurant that she is very sure was the agreed-upon meeting place, or she may have been sure that the time was two o'clock and not twelve. Jane may have been in a car accident, or perhaps her daughter got sick at school. She may have dialed my cell phone several times and received no answer for whatever reason. Jane may be angry at me for not being where and when she expected, or for failing to answer my cell phone. Even if Jane simply forgot our date, she is still not a villain—just a very normal, harried human being.

This is *not* about who is right and who is wrong. The point is about choosing happiness. As I sit at that empty table glancing at my watch, I can choose a happy story. It costs me nothing, and greatly increases the quality of my life. "Jane isn't here. I don't know why she isn't, but I choose to assume that she is OK and that our relationship is OK. I choose to be content in my *not knowing*."

Humans find it very difficult to *not know*. Our curious minds demand explanations and quickly invent painful stories whenever factual explanations are not immediately forthcoming. By short-circuiting the painful stories that we would otherwise have instinctively told ourselves, and intentionally choosing to remain in a trustful state of not knowing, we can experience joy rather than suffering.

Creating alternative stories for everything we see and hear is powerful and can protect us from the painful stories we compulsively tell ourselves.

Stories About Others

Yes, we do invent stories about *everything*. Sit in that busy coffeehouse and overhear the conversation at the next table. Your storytelling machine will be running full blast almost immediately.

It doesn't matter that you have never met those people—you are immediately imagining (telling yourself a story about) all kinds of details of these strangers' lives. Within the first minute, you know whether their relationships are solid and if their jobs are at risk. From there, you might fabricate details about their personal life, career, family, friends, and anything else that might come up. Yes, we all do it . . . all the time, even with family and friends.

We create even crazier stories about our family and friends. We have a history with them, and that history drives everything we think we see them do and hear them say. Our story about everything they do and say is so strongly biased that it barely resembles the video camera version.

TODAY IN MY WORLD:

As you go about life today, observe the story that you are creating in each moment, and then try on an alternative, happier story for each situation.

SHIP AND THE SEA: METAPHORS FOR LIFE

MAR The point of this book is that it's *your* life. Simply *Your Inspired Life* . . . but SYIL would not have made an appealing acronym. SAIL is much more provocative. Simply an Inspired Life. It's a lovely image of, perhaps, a sweet, colorful boat. It's at full sail in deep aqua blue water.

A life lived your best way. We share our stories and chart a course of clear and abiding principles that lighten the load and strengthen the journey. There are ways to embrace your days and make sense—short sense—out of the long non-sense of the world at large.

As you read this book with the spirit of an adventurer, these words will not, should not, tell you specific ways as to *how* you *should* live. Rather, these words are an invitation, a compass, to discover what directions these possibilities can take you. You will find challenge here to live an observed life, a life in which you are increasingly aware of those things that nudge you forward gently or with a forceful gale. We will wander in and out of sea metaphors. Create your own stories that resonate with your experiences, if sea metaphors do not grab your attention.

And be assured—I *do* want to grab your attention. So does Jonathan. He will speak inclusively, in the "we" of a classroom. I demonstrate through story and in the personal vernacular of my own experience.

I want to wake myself up, right along with you. Wake up to the amazing possibility of living joyful moments in the midst of challenge. Face difficulty or hardship with equanimity, ease, and grace. Wake up to profound perspective that allows me to celebrate the choices in each event and encounter. I want to awaken myself to a life where I recognize I am at the helm, *and* that I have no control. Awaken to the contradiction that only makes sense when I admit it makes no sense. I want to awaken you right along with me.

JLH SAIL is more than just an acronym for Simply an Inspired Life. A metaphoric SAILboat makes an ideal vehicle for our voyage through life's storms.

When life's storms rage, we respond best by turning their force to our own purposes—just as a physical sailboat redirects the force of the wind to create forward movement. Once we begin to think like a SAILboat, we can see life's storms as a power that we can utilize to design a bold and joyful life. When the winds of adversity blow strong, redirect their force into the service of your highest intention.

A friend says something, and I get upset—a small life-storm just hit me. My friend's remark is a *force*, like the wind, that I can redirect and use to power my intentions. One way of redirecting that force would be using it to trigger that long-delayed, deeply insightful conversation with my friend.

THE EIGHT POINTS OF *SIMPLY AN INSPIRED LIFE*

The Eight Points of *Simply an Inspired Life* are the touchstones that will guide our journey from suffering to joy:

- **Honor** for true self.
- **Forgiveness** for self and all.
- **Gratitude** in everything.
- **Choice** with open mind and heart.
- **Vision** with powerful intention.
- **Action** with bold courage.
- **Celebration** with joy.
- **Unity** with all creation.

The Eight Points of Simply an Inspired Life work together to enable us to take charge of the elements of our life with boldness and courage. Each point is essential to the process of SAILing—living Simply an Inspired Life.

For easy visualization, we associate the Eight Points with the eight spokes of a ship's wheel—the helm of the ship. Because taking command of a ship is called taking the helm, we describe taking full charge of life—especially the choices for joy or suffering—as *taking the helm on your life voyage.*

We established these eight points on the compass as a result of our own life experiences. Experiences that we observed, evaluated, shared, and synthesized. Perhaps you will want to shift these or identify/establish your own compass points as you read this book and determine what a simply inspired life looks like for you.

Consider making these affirmations of an inspired life a part of your daily expression of intent:

- **Honor**: I honor my true self.
- **Forgiveness**: I forgive myself and all others with

- Gratitude: I receive all of life with thanksgiving.
- ...se with open mind and open heart.
- Vision: I dream with powerful vision.
- ...with bold courage
- Celebration: I dance with a light heart.
- Unity: I am one with Spirit and all creation.

live boldly

laugh loudly

love truly

play as often as you can

work as smart as you are able

share your heart as deeply
as you can reach

choose in ways that
support your dreams

honor your actions
(perceived as success or
failure) as your teachers

as you awaken may your
dreams greet you by name
and may you answer, "yes!"

....as though your life
depended on it

live
Boldly

www.conari.com
www.maryanneradmacher.com

...ach of these Eight Points.
...ar, expectation, and dis-
...o a cycle of self-inflicted
...that cycle to regain our

Chapter 2

The Nature of Fear, Expectation, and Disappointment

Fear not the future, weep not for the past.
—Percy Bysshe Shelley

The past is wind at my back. It blew me here, but it does not govern me.

—mar

Where there is no accusation of fault, there can be no anger.

—jlh

JLH Life in its most predictable moments is a crazy quilt of suffering and joy. Fear, expectation, and disappointment add an uncertainty that tilts the balance inexorably toward suffering. We will all suffer, and we will all eventually die. The happenings of our lives are largely beyond our control. Our attitudes are the key to a joyful life. We can be in top physical shape, with a great job and a perfect family, and make ourselves miserable. Or, we can be in pain, near death, a widow or widower, and be joyful. The difference is in our attitude and perspective.

Our troubles are *real*, and we can't just wish them away—our pains hurt, our grief stings, and our compassion twinges when those around us suffer. We have troubles, and we also have many blessings. It is up to each of us to *choose* where we will focus our attention—on the troubles that cause us to suffer, or on the blessings that grant us great joy.

LIFE IS COMPOSED OF EVENTS AND FEELINGS

While greatly oversimplifying the complexities of life, we divide everything in our lives into two categories:

1. Events (every physical occurrence that, for whatever reason, has happened or is happening in our lives)
2. Feelings (our emotional reactions to events)

Category #1 (events) includes everything that happens outside our minds. It very specifically includes everything we say and everything that is said to us. It also includes tone of voice, facial expression, a headache, *everything* outside our minds. Everything that a video recorder could capture is in category #1, as is everything that could be physically measured—such as the nerve impulses of our headache or other physical pain, our heart rate, our tight muscles, our acid stomach.

What we call *thoughts* are really mostly emotional reactions. When our spouse says, "Can't you ever do anything right?" or our boss says, "You're late again," whatever thought we might believe we had in response isn't true thinking—it's a partially disguised emotional reaction to an event, and thus firmly in category #2.

Outside these categories lies true nonemotional thinking—such as when we are using our brains to formulate a theory of quantum gravity. However, all our suffering lies firmly within the two main categories—physical pain (for example, a toothache) in category #1, and emotional suffering in category #2.

Our principal focus in this book is on category #2. While we do have some control over what happens in our lives, in truth, we don't have a lot of control. To a large extent, life happens *to* us. We slip and fall, a parent sickens and dies, a lover leaves us, our company downsizes. Life happens *to* us in spite of our best efforts.

MAR I recently felt the full force of life happening *to* me. The population of the island on which I live had been struggling with nine days of snowfall. Ice. Treacherous roads. One Saturday afternoon there was a weather break, and hundreds of residents took the opportunity to go to the local grocery store and reinforce their supplies. The next storm would be moving over the island in a matter of hours. It was difficult to find a parking spot. The entire store was jammed, and the lines for each register stretched the length of the aisles. I took note of the responses around me. And my own response. I did not feel hurried. I shared tales, knowing glances, and reciprocal courtesies with fellow shoppers.

Then there were those who railed against the event. The resentment and inconvenience seethed from them. The laughter around them seemed to stir their angst even deeper. Several folks were simply streaming profanities under their breath.

Not one of us in that building could have any impact on the nature of the weather, present or incoming. We only had one front to govern: the weather of our hearts.

JLH While we have relatively little control over the physical occurrences of our lives—the broken leg, the death of a loved one—we *can* control our emotional response to these events. As a bonus, certain kinds of physical events—such as our tension headaches and acid stomach—will improve as a result of changing our emotional responses.

Whether we allow external events to shape our lives at a core level is very much within our own control—not by gritting our teeth and chanting "I'm OK, I'm OK, I'm OK," but by training ourselves to look at life from a more joyful point of view.

> **TODAY IN MY WORLD:**
>
> Today, whenever someone cuts you off in traffic, or otherwise triggers your upset, remind yourself that other people's actions are not directed against you personally. You are a minor character in their stories, as they are in yours.

The Anchor Between the What and the How

MAR The perspective I choose becomes the anchor for my sailboat in the midst of a gale. I choose the perspective when considering *what* has just happened *how* I will view it.

At the cusp of jumping back into the well-traveled course of self-inflicted suffering, I throw my anchor down. I pause.

I stop to observe and remind myself that while I do not govern all events, I do govern my perspective. My response. Participating in that pause allows SAIL to gently whisper in my ear, "Choose joy."

JLH It is human nature to complain. It might appear that our complaints come in unlimited variety, but every complaint fits neatly into one of only two categories: disappointment or fear. Disappointment is the emotion of suffering that we feel regarding the past and the present, while fear is the emotion that causes suffering whenever we consider our future.

FEAR—THE ROOT CAUSE OF OUR SUFFERING

Fear is the root of the tree of suffering.
—jlh

Fear is always about the future, and any suffering that relates to the future is always fear. We are never afraid of anything in the present or the past. What may appear to be fear of a past event is actually fear of the possibility that a similar (or worse) event may occur in the future. What appears to be fear of a present situation is actually fear that the current conditions will continue, worsen, or recur in the future.

Visualize taking a hike, hearing an ominous rattling sound, and looking down at the open jaws and forked tongue of a large poisonous snake exactly where you were about to step. Fear—cold, gripping fear. Yes, we are very afraid, but the fear is not about the present moment. We are perfectly safe and pain-free in this instant. The fear is about the future. Perhaps it is the future of two seconds from now, but still it is fear of the future.

Even if we are in extreme physical pain at this instant, our greatest suffering is fear of the future. We could stand any pain if we knew that it would end a second from now and not return.

The greatest suffering of physical pain is the fear that it will continue and perhaps intensify.

The Five Basic Fears

Although we have many different fears, we have only five gut-level instinctive fears:

1. Fear of the unknown, including death
2. Fear of physical pain
3. Fear of losing physiological necessities
4. Fear of attack and accident
5. Fear of abandonment

These five fears are an interesting mix. Fear of losing physiological necessities, such as food and air, and of attack and accident are clearly immediate survival issues. Physical pain and abandonment also relate to survival over a somewhat longer time frame. Someone in severe pain is unlikely to be able to care for herself. Abandonment is the loss of human companionship, which is essential for reproduction, and enables cooperation, greatly enhancing the probability of survival.

Fear of the unknown is, at first glance, the odd fear, but it's probably our greatest fear, and it has undoubtedly been intensified through evolution. Paranoia has had great survival value for the human species. Someone who is very afraid of everything becomes very careful, and lives longer—at least long enough to reproduce and nurture offspring. The ancestors of those who are alive today were the men and women who were very afraid of all the potential dangers and acted cautiously. Those who were fearless and foolhardy tended to die at a young age, before they could reproduce and pass on genes carrying their tendency toward fearlessness. The natural selection is invisible over a few generations, but becomes pronounced over many millennia.

> *What is not love is always fear, and nothing else.*
> —A Course in Miracles

MAR   Life experiences and responses are rooted in one of these two motivators: love or fear. This phrase is a core evaluative tool for me. It allows me to drop my anchor when I am headed toward choppy water, pause, and check in with my motivations. I am graced with a husband who reminds me of these two fundamental origins. It has become a familiar conversation between us. All we have to say is, "Love or fear?" It is an immediate and productive trigger for us to observe our own suffering. How can you see yourself begin to use this question?

TODAY IN MY WORLD:

Make a list of all your fears, such as:
- My spouse might leave me.
- I might get fired.
- I might get cancer.

Write down every fear. Next to each fear write the underlying instinctive fear:

1. The unknown
2. Physical pain
3. Losing physiological necessities
4. Personal attack and accident
5. Abandonment

Some higher-level fears trigger several instinctive fears. "He might leave me," triggers the instinctive fear of losing physiological necessities and probably of the unknown as well as of abandonment. The thought of being bullied or raped—two of our worst nightmares—trigger all five instinctive fears.

> If one of your fears doesn't seem to be related to any of the five instinctive fears, look deeper. You may have to step through several intermediate levels to get down to an instinctive fear.

Fear of Abandonment

JLH Most people can't even say the word *abandoned* without a cold shiver. We assume and expect that certain people—our parents, our spouse, and to some extent our children and our friends—will remain with us, stay loyal to us, and not abandon us. There is some logic for assuming that those close to us will remain loyal. On most days our spouse or parent doesn't move out. And on most days, our boss doesn't abandon us by saying, "You're fired." On the other hand, most people suffer at least one abandonment in their lifetime, so assuming loyalty isn't quite as rational as assuming the laws of nature will continue and the sun will rise tomorrow.

When our assumption and expectation of loyalty is breeched by an act of abandonment, we suffer disappointment and label the act an injustice. *Injustice* is just our word for "an unmet expectation."

Fear is always about the future. We are not afraid of an abandonment that occurred in the past, but our emotional reaction to that event does sensitize us to greater fear of potential future abandonments.

Look for a moment at the lengths we go to in order to retain companionship. Our techniques for enticing people to be our companions include: acting entertaining or funny, dressing or painting ourselves to appear more physically attractive, and performing services of all kinds for the other person. Our fear of abandonment and need for companionship can drive us to desperate acts that compromise our self-respect and even our safety. Observe that we simultaneously fear attack from other humans and fear being without them.

"Need"—Perceived Scarcity

Need is an especially ugly concept. The word *need* derives from an ancient Germanic word for "danger." When we first think of the word *need*, we don't tend to think first of danger, but keep it in mind as you read about need.

"You need to do that," and, "I need to do this," express a control emotion and a guilt emotion, respectively. "I need him," expresses a dependence emotion. "He always seems to need something," expresses a greed emotion. "I need it," may express addiction. "The starving people in Africa need food," expresses a struggle emotion. The word *need* is associated with a variety of emotions—none of them pleasant.

Need and fear cycle together in endless misery. We fear the lack of what we need—we need to avoid what we fear. To a middle-class twenty-first-century American, most of our fears of scarcity are leftovers from our ancestors' time, but to our emotional body, they are completely real. When our boss fires us, we feel a gut-level fear of scarcity. This instinctive fear of scarcity is almost completely independent of any underlying reality, and is just as real for the executive as for the janitor. The primal instincts of both scream, "No job means no food!"

We also suffer greatly over urgency—the perceived scarcity of time. "The deadline for my project at work is Monday. There's not enough time." What do I really fear? If my boss or coworkers don't approve of my work, I could lose their respect, which could, in turn, cause the loss of my job. Ultimately this represents core issues of food and human companionship. And, if I work on the project instead of having dinner with my wife and watching my son's soccer game, I head down a different path that also ends with the core issue of human companionship.

Time, respect, and a thousand other perceived must-haves can be reduced to five core needs.

The Five Core Needs

The nature of being human is to feel the need for five basic conditions—and to live in the constant fear of their loss.

—jlh

There are only five basic human needs—five conditions that we instinctively seek:

1. Certainty
2. Freedom from pain
3. Survival
4. Safety
5. Human companionship

They are a one-to-one match with our five basic fears. These are the five basic need/fear pairs:

1. Need for certainty	Fear of the unknown
2. Need for comfort	Fear of physical pain
3. Need for survival	Fear of losing necessities
4. Need for safety	Fear of personal danger
5. Need for companionship	Fear of abandonment

For middle-class Americans, our instinctive needs have become more an issue of perception than of reality—yet we fear for our safety and survival with the same gut-level instincts that our ancestors did.

Our gut doesn't do math. However low the numerical probability of bodily harm to ourselves or our families, we are afraid of another 9/11, a hurricane, a serial rapist, a child molester in the neighborhood, a shark attack. People always seem to settle into a certain level of fear, independent of the level of actual danger. When food is scarce or bombs are dropping, we overlook the possibility that our neighbor might seduce our child—but when greater urgencies fade away, we become obsessed by that possibility.

Our Perceived Need for Respect and Approval

We come by the need for respect and approval naturally. We want to be like other people—at least we want to be like other people whom we admire—and we want other people to like and approve of us.

Today, our physical survival does not depend upon the respect and approval we earn. Our modern value system requires that everyone be fed regardless of whether they are respected, and independent of their ability to repay the kindness. But it wasn't always that way. In times long past, your fellow humans would only care for you in times of need or infirmity if you had previously cared for them, or if they believed you could and would care for them in the future. Our emotional body remembers, and still reacts to the loss of respect and approval as a life-threatening issue.

Having said all that, our need for respect and approval is not a core need, but rather a behavior (or manipulation) that humans use to gain the core needs of human companionship, safety, survival, and certainty. In order to attract the companionship of other humans, we behave bravely to gain respect, we enhance our physical attractiveness, and we offer food and other gifts. At a core level, we humans don't much care what we have to do to gain human companionship and our other core needs—as long as we succeed.

> **TODAY IN MY WORLD:**
> Make a list of the people from whom you need love, approval, and appreciation. What form of approval do you need from each? Contemplate your answers.

Assumption and Expectation—They're Not the Same

In this book, we make a crucial distinction between the concept "assumption" and the concept "expectation."

For us, as for a dictionary, an assumption is a guess, belief, or hope, without any factual basis, that something is true or that something will occur.

If you look in a dictionary, you will find several definitions for the word "expectation," including it being a synonym for assumption. In this book, however, we use the word "expectation" in only one way. The sense in which we use *expectation* is: a (possibly implicit) demand for an action based on an *assumed* obligation.

Remember that assumptions are beliefs, while expectations are demands.

Expectation

By nature, we are creatures of habit, foreboding, and hope. We are generally unskilled at responding to completely unforeseen events—even when those events might otherwise bring us great comfort and joy. As a result, we attempt to standardize our world with rules of how people should behave, and we demand that everyone follow those rules. This maximizes our suffering when people and nature fail to meet our rules, which is a frequent occurrence.

MAR I am amazed at the number of times this habit of rule making sneaks up on the back door of my experience. I'll be involved in something, completely unaware that I've already written a set of rules for it. Unaware, that is, until I encounter disappointment from some element of the event not following my sense of rule, or unidentified expectation.

When asked about the turnout of an event we have been excited about, our answer is often apathetic. "It was . . . okay. Um, I mean, you know, it was an okay deal. I just thought there was going to be a lot more. . . ." And the rest of the conversation will be filled with what we thought the process was going to be, and what it wasn't. Rarely do we celebrate how something completely surprises us, how it totally stumps our expectations and takes us into an entirely new and fresh arena. As Jonathan has and will point out, absolute surprise isn't generally on the top of anyone's secret expectation hit parade. Expectations are well-kept secrets—even we who hold them are unaware they are sitting there, just waiting for the opportunity to disappoint us.

Expectation—a (possibly implicit) demand for an action based on an assumed (believed) obligation.

JLH We can begin to see the treacherous nature of expectation just from its dictionary definition. *Obligation* isn't a great beginning. Most of us instinctively cringe at the idea of being obligated to others or having them obligated to us. Same with *demand.* We don't want to be demanding, and we surely don't want to have demanding people in our lives. The subtle dangers to our emotional well-being get even greater when we include the insidious words *implicit* and *assumed.*

Expectations aren't straightforward requests or clearly stated demands. They are camouflaged mind tricks—slimy propositions at best. Worse, they are typically disguised in seemingly mild-mannered but treacherous phrases such as "I need to..." or "You're supposed to..."

MAR Expectation is also partnered with repetition. Repetition is a natural breeding ground for expectation. I have seen this in my capacity as a community volunteer. If you've experienced this, you'll be nodding your head wildly in a boy-ain't-that-the-truth kind of way.

One year the community organization is stumped. At the eleventh hour a committee head has been unexpectedly and immediately relocated due to his wife's job transfer. I step in. "I'll pick this up." I'm celebrated as a hero. I do an exemplary job, and everyone is thrilled. Several months later—it's time to make that committee assignment again. I say, "No, thank you for asking." The disappointment is present all around the table. The objections start flying.

"What do you mean, no?"

"You stepped in last year, and it was perfect. No one can do this better than you. We just figured since you were so good at it, you would do it again."

Ah. It would be awesome if we could build a warning system when these types of things are presented. Accepting a committee assignment under the cloak of these types of rules, expectations, and assumptions will lock the assignment in—ah—community service cement.

Assumption—Cultural Belief

Assumption—a guess, belief, or hope, without any factual basis, that something is true or that something will occur.

JLH The difference between opinion and assumption is that opinions are conscious beliefs while assumptions are implicit. When we state our opinions, we leave room for others to hold differing opinions—when we state our assumptions, we present them as absolute fact and are surprised and angry when others do not share them.

In addition to carrying our fears and needs, we are also burdened by our assumptions about the nature of the world. Unlike our fears and needs, which are instinctive and universal, assumptions are a function of our culture—mostly the beliefs of our family, friends, and community. Assumptions come in all flavors: "The earth is round," "The earth is flat," "We should welcome strangers," "We should build a big fence." Those assumptions that cause our suffering are called *limiting assumptions.*

Limiting assumptions are mostly statements about what *should* and what *shouldn't* happen, and what we and those around us *need to do* and *must not do.*

In addition to having assumptions about what we need to have, we also have assumptions about what we and others need to do—that is, obligations—the ways in which we are obligated to others and others are obligated to us. Recognizing our assumptions about obligation is key to relieving our suffering.

The first step to conquering assumption and expectation is to become aware of just what assumptions and expectations we actually have about life. They are seldom attitudes that we have consciously chosen. Almost always, they have grown on us over the years—like mold in a stale, dark closet.

Assumptions at Home

When I first began my writing career, I looked around the house for an appropriate place to support my creativity. Perhaps this corner. Perhaps conscripting a guest bedroom. I was completely unaware of the magnitude of the limitations that I was imposing on my choice of a home for my writing.

I was conscious of a few of my self-imposed limitations (assumptions). As I considered using a guest bedroom to host my writing, I was aware of questioning my self-worth. Did I deserve a dedicated writing room? Would I have the perseverance to justify that level of commitment? What about guests? Weren't we supposed to have a guest bedroom?

I never said to myself, "A house is supposed to have a living room and a dining room and a kitchen and a master bedroom and a guest bedroom and . . ." I never said anything like that, because that was an *assumption*—a self-imposed limitation of which I was completely unaware. It was just there—assumed—like gravity, like water to a fish.

My wonderfully supportive wife, Suze, said, "Let's move the dining table into the living room in front of the window to use as a work table, and we'll move one of the couches into the dining room to make it a sitting area."

But, but, but!? was my reaction. My unconscious assumption about what a real home is supposed to look like had been pulled out of its dark closet and was thrust into the light of day—where it lay looking pale and scrawny.

"Oh, I never thought of that," was what I said, but what I meant was, *Oh my God, I'm not worth it, and that's not how a real home is supposed to look, and what about that dream cottage with the white picket fence that I promised you, and I feel so guilty when you're so generous, and what about guests, and why was I too closed-minded to think of that, and . . .*

What are your assumptions about your home? How big of a home do you assume you need, and why? What would be the most practical way to furnish and use your rooms if tradition and convention weren't issues? What are your assumptions about your car? Your job? Your clothes? Household chores? Vacations? Everything else in your life?

Think of a time when your assumptions and expectations about something or someone were shattered. Was the experience devastating or educational? Imagine the power of seeking out some of your assumptions and expectations and intentionally blowing them up.

Disappointment

Disappointment is the inevitable result of expectation. We are disappointed whenever life doesn't live up to our expectations— whether the cause is other people, ourselves, or the vicissitudes of nature. If we didn't have expectations, we wouldn't have disappointments and we would avoid a huge amount of suffering.

Look at the sequence of expectation, disappointment, and suffering in the following example.

I expect that my cell phone will work reliably wherever and whenever I want. I expect that at all times it will support incoming and outgoing calls to anywhere in the world, send and receive e-mail, show a map of where I am and directions to wherever I want to go, search virtually all the world's information in a fraction of a second, manage my to-do list, and play free music of my choice. Whenever service is interrupted, I am disappointed and I suffer. Whether I wandered outside the coverage area, the phone company had an outage, the battery ran down, the cell phone itself had a hardware or software oops, or I dropped the device,

I am disappointed and suffer (greatly) whenever my cell phone stops working.

Expect is such a concept! Think for a moment about "I expect my cell phone to work." Wow! Where do I get off *expecting* cell phone service? I have lived most of my life without cell phones of any kind—anyone else remember rotary dial telephones? Talk about Self-Inflicted Suffering. I *suffer* when my cell phone stops working? It's crazy for at least two reasons. First, a cell phone is a luxury, and humans did fine without cell phones for the first three million years. Second, I know from past experience that my cell phone will fail again, I just don't know exactly when and where. Why would I choose to suffer over something that is a pure indulgence and that I know is subject to failure?

I hear you saying, "But I need my cell phone for business calls." Just take a step back and listen to yourself. *Need?* Think of perceived scarcity and core needs, and remember the danger in need.

Holding expectations always increases suffering as compared to having no expectations. This is true whether we believe that our expectations will be met or that they will not be met. This is also true whether our expectations are actually met or not.

MAR Expectations are like germs. They are everywhere. The way you manage your view of expectation is the way you wash your hands of them.

Who, Me?

JLH Each of us is the proud owner of numerous assumptions and expectations which limit our thinking and our range of action, and of which we are completely unaware.

We can't just snap our fingers, say, "I think I'll become aware today," and have our limiting assumptions and expectations show up in sharp focus. What we can do is first accept that we are overflowing with limiting assumptions and expectations even when we are not aware of them.

Second, we can be open to having a light shined on our assumptions and expectations. When circumstances, our friends, or even our enemies highlight our limiting assumptions and expectations, we can question them rather than just defending them.

TODAY IN MY WORLD:

This exercise has three parts that explore the three aspects of assumed obligation—the obligations you feel toward others, the obligations you believe others have toward you, and the obligations you believe people have to society.

List at least ten things you did today. For each item, identify whether you did it because you chose to do it, or because you needed to do it. For those items with which you associated *needed,* write down the authority that imposed the necessity—God, society, your boss, your spouse, yourself. . . . Contemplate why you gave up your conscious attention and free will to that authority. If you had made a truly freewill choice about each of the needed items, would you have either done different things today or felt differently about doing them?

List at least ten things others did for you today. Remember to include the seemingly invisible services, such as those performed by all the people who keep your electricity flowing. For each item, identify whether they performed a service for you because they chose to do it as a freewill gift, or because you demanded (expected) that they do it. For each item (other than those marked as freewill gifts), write down the authority that imposed the obligation—God, society, your company, your family, yourself. . . . Contemplate why you believe that each person is obligated to provide you with this service. If you had been truly conscious about each of your expectations, how might you have behaved or felt differently today?

List at least ten things others did or failed to do today that caused you disappointment. An example would be your expectation that everyone should recycle, and your disappointment at seeing someone throw a soda can into the garbage. For each item, write down the authority that imposed the obligation—God, society, your company, your family, yourself . . . Contemplate why you believe people are obligated to meet your personal expectations of behavior.

RED-FLAG PHRASES

Assumption and expectation are sometimes stated directly ("I assume that . . ." "I expect you to . . ."), but more frequently they are concealed insidiously in common phrases, which we call red-flag phrases.

The red-flag phrases for expectation include:

You should . . .
I have to . . .
You ought to . . .
I can't . . .
Would you . . .
I need to . . .
You're supposed to . . .

Can you hear the expectation in each of those phrases? "Would you take out the garbage, honey?" is not a question.

A couple of possibly surprising red-flag words for expectation are *always* and *never.* Visualize being on the receiving end of "You never remember to take out the garbage," or "You always talk too much." There is a strong expectation in both cases.

Assumption is a lot harder to detect in common speaking. Red-flag phrases for assumption are *is* statements that contain comparatives. *Good* and *bad* are obvious comparatives, as in, "Tuna fish is bad for you."

Some comparatives are well hidden. When someone says, "Los Angeles is a dangerous place," it is shorthand for, "Los Angeles is a *more* dangerous place than . . ." which makes it an *is* statement with a comparative.

A few of the many other comparatives that warn of the presence of assumption are:

truth	lie
right	wrong
win	lose
succeed	fail
better	worse

Urgency Phrases Get a Double Red Flag

When we hear that something is urgent, that statement deserves a double red flag. "That report is due tomorrow" sends a message of urgency, but worse, it contains both an assumption and an expectation. The assumption lies in presenting someone's opinion of the importance of completing that report as absolute truth. The expectation is the implicit demand that someone, probably you, is obligated to produce that report as commanded by some implied authority in adherence to some implied rule.

When you hear red-flag phrases, it's time to become cautious. When such words come out of your own mouth, listen and start ringing the alarm bells.

You may have noticed that this book uses red-flag phrases such as *always* and *never*—what's going on? Red-flag phrases warn that an opinion is being expressed. There is nothing wrong with opinions—the entire content of this book consists of the opinions of the authors. We are very clear that we are stating our opinions—don't believe anything we say; use what we say as a springboard for your own inquiry of your life, your values, your future. The danger of red-flag phrases occurs when opinions are stated as absolute truth, in which case they become hidden assumptions, which preclude the free exchange of true opinions and cause limitless suffering.

BREAKING THE CYCLE OF SELF-INFLICTED SUFFERING

We live our lives in an endless Cycle of Self-Inflicted Suffering. The elements of this cycle are our most fundamental emotions, and they are tightly interwoven. We discussed fear, expectation, and disappointment individually. Now we bring the elements together as they interact in our cycle of suffering.

In the Cycle of Self-Inflicted Suffering, there are four stages that repeat continuously throughout our lifetime—unless we break the cycle:

1. We enter the cycle with our fears, our perceived needs, and our assumed obligations. We assume (believe) that

we know what our obligations are to others, and what their obligations are to us.

2. Based on our fears, perceived needs, and assumed obligations, we develop expectations of ourselves and for how others should relate to us—the "I should," "you must," "I have to," "you're supposed to," and "I need to" that demand adherence to the rules that (we assume) define the nature of our world.

3. We suffer disappointment. The expectations we have of ourselves, our companions, and the world at large can never be met, and we are always disappointed.

4. We become angry and resentful, and we blame those to whom we attribute fault for the injustice. We feel guilt and shame for our own actions and inactions. We also develop additional assumptions about the nature of our world. All this causes renewed fear that the future will continue to be painful and perhaps will become even more painful, and this leads us back to the beginning of the cycle, where we fear the next event in our lives.

The cave you fear to enter holds the treasure you seek.
—Joseph Campbell

Happiness cannot thrive within the prison of obligation.
—jlh

Which came first, the chicken or the egg? It's not a meaning-ful question because chickens laying eggs and eggs growing into chickens form an endless cycle. Each event causes the next—for-ever. The Cycle of Self-Inflicted Suffering is like that. Fear causes suffering, and suffering causes fear in an endless cycle. While this relationship is not immediately apparent, we will not only examine this cycle, but reveal how to break the cycle and gain access to a joyful life.

You can move beyond suffering by breaking the Cycle of Self-Inflicted Suffering.

What are the weakest phases of the cycle—the points where the cycle is most vulnerable to being broken?

Fear, anger, resentment, blame, guilt, and shame all contain a major component of instinct. Later, we will address transforming these instincts, but they are not the weak link.

Disappointment is the result of expectation, and expectation is the result of fears, needs, and obligations. Therefore, disappointment and expectation are also not the weakest points in the cycle.

That leaves perceived needs (what you "need" to have) and assumed obligations (what you "need" to do) as the weak links of the cycle. They can be addressed through conscious questioning, thus breaking the cycle.

One way to break the cycle is to question what you think you need to have. If you need less, you then expect less, are less disappointed, are less resentful, and are less fearful that your needs will not be met in the next repetition of the cycle.

Why bother to suffer over what you don't have but think you need?

TODAY IN MY WORLD:

Ask yourself some questions about what you need:

- What do I really need?
- What do I need so much that I choose to suffer if I don't get it?
- Might I be more joyful if I didn't need as much?

There is nothing that any of us ever needs to have. When you say that you *need* to have something or *need* to do something, you are expressing a belief that you have no choice in the matter. Regardless of the circumstances, you *always* have a choice.

Needs are not real—only actions and their consequences are. For example, an alcoholic might say, "I need a drink." That statement likely conveys a true conviction that there is no choice in the matter—a desperation that has a very different character from a more rational, "If I don't get a drink soon, I will suffer uncontrollable shaking and vomiting, and will suffer greatly."

Remember the connection between need and danger. When one feels a strong need, one senses danger and becomes desperate. Sometimes the intensity of the desperation and the severity of the consequences are in balance, as when a person lost in the desert feels desperation for water, and the consequence of not finding water is likely death.

Often, however, the compulsive craving and the consequences of not fulfilling the perceived need are out of balance or even inverted. Let's look at our perceived need for food. Food is part of the third perceived need (survival) in the list of five core needs we discussed earlier. While we all perceive a need for food, and are afraid of being denied food, the consequences of not having this need met vary with the circumstances. For a malnourished person, the consequence of not eating when they feel an instinctive need for food is death. For an obese person, however, resisting the siren song of that compulsive need is the key to a healthy lifestyle.

We believe that we have needs primarily for two reasons—instincts and habits. We are born with what we have labeled "the five core needs." Through our family and community we develop an additional list of what we perceive as "needs." These culturally defined perceived needs vary widely. For a sub-Saharan African herdsman, perceived needs might include a goat and cloth. For a middle-class American, they typically include an automobile and a credit card.

The secret here is to break the habit of neediness and to still the plaintive cries: my neighbor just bought a new car, my co-worker just got a raise, and my brother just went on a cruise . . . "It's just not *fair.*"

Your choice is whether to live your life in the complaint that it's just not fair or to choose to be thankful for what you have and to be joyful. Breaking the Cycle of Self-Inflicted Suffering depends on that choice. Life is *not* fair, and you can still choose joy.

BEYOND ASSUMED OBLIGATIONS

The easiest way to break the Cycle of Self-Inflicted Suffering is to question the reality of the obligations that you assume to exist—your obligations to others, the obligations of others to you, and the obligations of others to society. If you reduce the number and intensity of the obligations that you assume to exist, you then expect less, are disappointed less, are less resentful, and are less fearful that your assumed obligations will not be met on the next repetition of the cycle.

Your first task is to identify what you assume you are obligated to do for others, and what you assume others are obligated to do for you and for the world. This task of identifying your assumed obligations is much harder than it might seem, because you are usually blind to your own assumptions.

Refer back to the lists you made in the Expectations of You and the Your Expectations of Others exercises for clues to identifying assumed obligations. After identifying them, you can begin to question and possibly alter your assumed obligations.

Why bother to suffer over what you *assume* you need to do? Why bother to suffer over what you believe others need to do—either specifically for you or for the world?

The secret to moving past what you believe you need to do is to examine where your assumed obligations originated. Most frequently, they began with your parents, your religion, or your community.

"I need to have a good job." There is a lot of assumption in what makes a job good, and in what a job is, as well as the need to have a job at all. Start asking yourself questions. Why do I choose to work? Perhaps because I want my job to provide money, satisfaction, pleasant interpersonal interaction, an opportunity to learn, and a challenge. Which of those desires does my current job provide? Hopefully the answer is, "all of them," but suppose the answer is, "just money." Will just money make me happy? Isn't it my duty to work hard even if I hate my job? Why? I need the money. How much money do I need? I've got a big mortgage and I'm still paying on both my cars. How much money do I really need? You aren't suggesting that I downsize, are you? What have I always wanted to do? Perhaps do woodworking. Suppose I sold my big house and bought a smaller one with a shop in back, you don't really think I could make a living that way, do you? The essential question is always: What choices in life will bring me joy while keeping me nourished and healthy? Why not move directly to that question and eliminate all the assumed obligations?

The secret to moving past your assumptions of others' obligations toward you is to throw away your whole concept of fair.

"I did the dishes; you need to take out the garbage."

"You borrowed money from me; you need to pay it back."

"It's not fair."

When life occurs differently from the way you wish, you can inflict great suffering upon yourself by complaining about life being unfair. You can get angry, complain, or attempt revenge—perhaps violently. But life is not fair, and you can't make it fair.

Life consists of actions and reactions, events and feelings, not fairness and unfairness. *Fair* is not even a useful concept. Fair is a *fairy* tale. Life is *not* fair!

The instant you give up your assumption that life is supposed to be fair, you break the Cycle of Self-Inflicted Suffering. Once you give up your assumption that life is supposed to be fair, you no longer have any expectations. Having no expectations, you are no longer subject to disappointment. And once you no longer experience disappointment, you no longer blame anyone for anything. Further, you no longer fear that life will be unfair next time, because you no longer hold the assumption that life *should* be fair.

TODAY IN MY WORLD:

Finally, question your beliefs about how others are obligated to behave in the world:

- How do I really need others to behave?
- On whose authority am I demanding that they behave as I prefer?
- What are the consequences to me when they behave as they prefer?
- In what ways do I need others to behave so much that I choose to suffer when they behave otherwise?
- Might I be more joyful if I didn't feel the need to control the behavior of others?

The secret to moving past your assumptions of others' obligations for behavior in the world is illustrated by Byron Katie's observation that not everything is your business, and that "there are only three kinds of business in the universe: mine, yours, and God's."

When you demand that others behave as you prefer, you are minding their business and God's business. They are not going to do what you want simply because you want it. Sometimes, by chance, they will happen to make the choices you are demanding, but often they will not, and you will be upset and suffer. For example, you think your brother-in-law should stop smoking. Whether he smokes is his business, not yours. It is not in your power to choose whether he smokes. What is in your power is the choice of whether his habit causes *you* to suffer. Choose joy—mind only your own business.

Life is not supposed to be fair.

—jlh

MAR Break the cycle of your self-inflicted suffering. Increase your observation of and awareness about those unwritten and often undisclosed rules in your life. Use as many of these exercises as you want to become your anchor, your pause at the start of yet another cycle of suffering. Create a new pattern. A new way that empowers you, regardless of circumstance, to literally captain—to take the helm—on the ship of your life. Break the limiting process of suffering, and you will begin the full embrace of a life that is simply inspired.

Chapter 3
HONOR—For True Self

AFFIRMATION I Honor My True Self—I grant myself the honor of being me. I am unique in all time and space. I am beyond perceived scarcity, obligation, and the need for approval. I am honored that Spirit has chosen to create me. ॐ

The greatest way to live with honor in this world is to be what we pretend to be.

—Socrates

Honor yourself with lovingly courageous actions chosen intentionally.

—mar

Honor your being,
Release each and every struggle,
Gather strength from life's storms,
Relax into the arms of spirit.

—jlh

JLH   Access to the happiness of Simply an Inspired Life is gained in two very different but complementary ways—one transformative, the other habitual. Breaking the Cycle of Self-Inflicted Suffering is transformative. In a flash you comprehend that life is joyful because there is nothing to fear and nothing you ever need to have or need to do. If you have already had that revelation, congratulations! If not, don't lose hope, the seeds have been planted. When you least expect, you will just *get* it.

The other means of access to Simply an Inspired Life is changing your habitual patterns—learning to stop doing those things that cause you to suffer, and developing daily patterns of emotionally healthy behavior. The Eight Points of Simply an Inspired Life provide access to changing your daily habits of emotionally self-destructive behavior into habits that support your happiness and growth. We invite you to explore the Eight Points, beginning with *honor for true self.*

MAR   Don't wait. For some of you, these words are all you need. Don't wait. You know exactly what I mean.

The finest stationery in the back of your drawer. The tools that you don't let the kids touch. Special occasion stuff that you hardly ever have occasions special enough to touch.

Don't wait.

The love you hold in your heart that you *know* they know so why bother saying it? The kiss, the lingering touch, the hug, the appreciation of your family, your friends, and most significantly, your *self.*

Say it. Don't wait. Begin honoring yourself.

Remember the dream you've held for so long? The one that you wish for while you are doing the other stuff? The dream that you think you don't have enough money for, aren't yet smart enough to do, or do not have the courage to do? *That* dream?

Begin it.

The person you want to meet. The individual you want to praise, congratulate, honor? The friend you want to reconnect with. The person you have waited to apologize to . . . the relationship you ought to rebuild but keep waiting. The fitness program you keep waiting for a convenient time to begin. The closet that haunts your mornings because it's so crammed full of stuff that you don't use but don't have the guts to give away.

Don't wait.

The path to honoring yourself begins as you start on your dreams, your impulses, your longings, your special occasions. Today *is* your moment. You aren't going to be any smarter, more ready, more able, or more qualified than you are right now.

Now is the time in my life when I choose to live fearlessly. When I get to stand in the wind of uncertainty and lean forward. When I get to put the money of dreams where the mouth of my actions are and make my creative life expand and explode. I've looked in the mirror and said, "Don't wait."

I'm not going to. What about you?

The colors and rich ways of the world around you invite you in all ways, to SAIL into your life, your dreams, your best self.

HONOR'S JOURNEY HOME
Honor knows so many roads. . . . When met with
disappointment, honor whispers hope. When
confronted with anger, it listens harder. When

faced with challenge, honor imagines fiercely. When approached with harm, it raises an open palm. When utterly betrayed, honor knows to walk away tall. When loving unconditionally, honor knows to thrive. When touched by appreciation, honor basks in gratitude. When shown a new way, honor becomes a student. When cornered, honor finds a way to continue the journey home. Honor finds its greatest joy as a gift given truly.

WHAT IS HONOR?—WHAT IS HONOR OF SELF?

JLH The small dictionary I just opened has twenty definitions for *honor,* so clearly we are going to be focusing on a very special aspect of honor. "Esteem," "respect," "admire," and "value" come closest to the aspect of honor that I am addressing. When I honor myself, I respect, admire, and value myself.

Another definition for *honor* is "pride," and pride has a very mixed reputation. Before we return to honor as "respect," "admire," and "value," let's take a look at the dual nature of pride.

Pride: Self-Honor or Self-Importance?

Pride has a Dr. Jekyll and Mr. Hyde quality. Just look at two definitions:

1. satisfaction with self; the satisfied feeling of having achieved something that other people admire.
2. ego; self-importance; feeling of superiority; a haughty attitude; the (unjustified) belief that one is better than others.

Pride, as in self-importance, is on the list of *seven deadly sins,* and the Bible doesn't speak well of pride: 1 Samuel 2:3—"Do not keep talking so proudly or let your mouth speak such arrogance." James 4:6—"God opposes the proud but gives grace to the humble."

Ironically, an attitude of exaggerated self-importance originates from low self-esteem rather than as an expression of high self-value. This combination of low self-esteem and exaggerated self-importance causes great suffering to everyone around as well as to the person so burdened.

Pride in the favorable sense shows up when someone says something like: "I'm proud to be an American," or "I'm proud of what I have accomplished." We are likely to think highly of a person who expresses those sentiments.

Where is the boundary between a healthy appreciation of the gifts one has been given or the tasks one has completed, and the onset of looking down on others?

TODAY IN MY WORLD:

Write "I am proud because . . ." and make a list of the reasons you are proud. Now write "I am more talented or more successful than my family and my friends because . . ." and make a list of reasons. Compare the two lists. What did you learn from this exercise?

Bring Honor to Yourself

MAR Choose joy. Just two words. A powerful instruction. Many books have been written identifying the diverse roads to joy. Choose joy. It's a simple directive. Some would argue with commonsense philosopher Abraham Lincoln. They say choosing joy is complex, requiring substantial value assessments and complete reorientation of priorities. Mr. Lincoln, tied to his own complex set of difficulties and sadnesses which he faced throughout his life, might turn and say, "I reckon people are as happy or joyful as they make up their minds to be."

I honor myself by choosing joy. Today. This moment. I will not delay my reward to the end of all the things I believe I have to do, the things that my to-do list instructs me that I must do. I, who have written, "Do the difficult thing first," recognize that is sometimes the most effective way to approach a day. Eleanor Roosevelt taught me that I must do the thing I think I cannot do. I expanded her lesson to include the difficult thing I simply don't want to do. Do it first. Get it out of the way. I clean up the room for joy . . . I get rid of the thing I'm dreading.

More to the point is this: Stop dreading the *thing*. Whatever it is. Choose joy. If all of our lives are a matter of perspective (and they are), then I can bring to whatever task whatever attitude I wish.

I delay providing myself my greatest joy—using my joys and pleasures like the proverbial carrot on the end of a stick—to get my inner racing dog to run faster, ace out the competition and get to the finish line first.

In choosing joy, the finish line dissolves into a different concept altogether. "The things that matter" are discussed in the large discourse, in the "bigger picture," our view of our personal mission. In the daily process here's what happens: the things that don't matter often win. Those small things that we do because they are easier, prevail.

They are more immediate and have a distinct sense of satisfaction attached to them. I call those activities cookies. Little bite-size cookies. Why? I observe that when I diet, I tend to abstain from large pieces of anything delicious. Big cookies, honkin' brownies, giant slices of cake. Ah—but the little cookie. It's as if, somehow, by its simple diminished size, the calories are remarkably absent. And the grand diet scheme that allowed for no sweets somehow made way for the little cookies.

So it is in our days. The sweet, little, quick, and achievable things lay claim to the currency of our dreams, our aspirations, and our joys. At day's end, the reward that was earlier promised, quid pro quo, is not available because the things on the list were not first accomplished. There is a defensive explanation—have you heard this? "I did get a lot done, just none of it was what I thought." And where's the satisfaction in that? There can be reward in the anticipated tasks, and it is important that we pay attention to the things we identify as important. Honor the expressed priorities.

Bringing honor to myself allows for clarity for my joys. Working toward my greater vision by first identifying and realizing what that greater vision is. Honor for myself means that I can reward myself immediately, in a variety of ways. I reward myself with a joyful and satisfying activity simply because I rose, with purpose, to greet my day.

The events of the day will unfold with or without my permission. Just because an opportunity comes knocking on my door (the door of my day, the door of my to-do list) does not mean I have to utilize that opportunity. A declining statement requiring clarity is, "Not now. Not ever." I can say, "Not now," or "Later—right now I'm investing the currency of my spirit in my own joy." Opportunities can dress up quite nicely—but that doesn't mean you have to go out with them!

The most precious commodity you have is your time. You are making an assessment as to how you will spend it, invest it, utilize it. If you were investing actual cash capital—all your options would come under consideration and the anticipated results measured before you would lay your cash on the counter. And yet—as joy is considered—the purchase rate becomes negotiable, reduced, or traded away.

Choose joy. Reward yourself immediately and as an incentive. Recognize that personal worth is determined by what we hold in our spirit, not what we hold in our hands or our portfolios or on our shelves or walls. The capacity to embrace all the events of my day and recognize them for the joy they hold lives within. Sometimes embracing the events of a day means rearranging a priority. Honoring what is important means being flexible and present.

Lincoln made it through his emotionally demanding life by honoring himself and choosing his own joy. I do too. How about you?

JLH A to-do list can be a useful memory tool. Write tasks on it, do the tasks, check them off. The dangerous to-do list is the one that lingers. For each task that needs to be done, either choose to do it soon and forget it, or choose to purge it forever from your need-to-do list. An obligation that lingers is a wearisome burden.

RESPECTING MYSELF

Rarely is it a conscious choice to dishonor and disrespect ourselves—we just fall into lifelong patterns that increasingly fail to honor our being.

In a hypothetical example, my friend Judy opened her own store last year, but she has yet to turn a profit. She keeps the store open seven days a week and spends late evenings searching the Web for new products to carry. She brings a smile to our breakfast support group.

My other friend Cathy comes to the breakfast with a sour look even though she just got a raise and now makes twice as much as most people at the table. "They just don't appreciate me. I deserved a promotion."

So which friend is actually paying to work, and which friend would generally be considered well paid? You would never guess from their faces. It's not about money, and it's not about time. It's about self-respect and self-worth.

It is (relatively) easy to sit down to coffee or have a drink with a friend, listen to their story, and know what they "should" do to fix their life. We might say: "Quit that lousy job. You can find a better one tomorrow."

Now sit in the other seat. We tell our friend how badly our spouse or boss is treating us, and then we bristle when our friend says, "Just leave the jerk."

"But, but, but . . ." we start. "The kids and I need a home—do you expect us to just live on the street?" or "I need my job—do you think I can just find another job tomorrow?"

When our friends tell us something like, "Just leave the jerk," they are actually paying us a huge compliment. Without directly saying so, they are conveying their confidence that we are capable of living on our own and that we will find a way to function successfully without that deadbeat spouse or dead-end job.

What if we had as much confidence in our own survival abilities as our friends do?

I am not suggesting that the best way to handle difficult situations is always—or even usually—to leave. The possibility of triggering the final break in a fragile relationship is simply one of the risks we take whenever we stand up for ourselves. Whatever choices you make about relationships or anything else, make those choices from a position of self-respect and never from a perceived need to have something or from a perceived need to do, or avoid doing, something.

In reality, we never *need* to do anything. Each action we take, each thought we think, and each emotion we feel is a choice— whether a conscious choice made with full awareness or a choice made in the fog of habitual instinct. If we decide to stay in a dead-end job or relationship rather than making the sacrifices necessary to upgrade our career or living situation, it is a *choice*—conscious or not.

> **TODAY IN MY WORLD:**
>
> Look at your friends. Whose lives appear to be working well? What characteristics are shared among joyful successful lives, and what characteristics are shared among lives of suffering? Are the *need-to-have* and the *need-to-do* lists defining elements of their lives?

Honor Is Courageous, Heroic, and Joyful

When I think of courage, I visualize Heroes—with big capital Hs on their chests. Heroes are courageous and self-reliant, and they are greatly admired. Courage and self-reliance are among the qualities that define heroes. Being admired comes afterward.

Genuine heroes always walk their own path. They may or may not lead other people, but all heroes lead themselves. Heroes are self-confident, independent thinkers who make courageous choices. By committing their entire focus to their goals, heroes leave no time or energy for worry or self-inflicted emotional suffering. Heroism is a path to a joyful life as well as to inspired service.

> **TODAY IN MY WORLD:**
>
> Consider a list of famous people and contemplate why you do or do not consider each of them heroic. Who is your personal greatest hero? Write why you admire your greatest hero. Which of his or her qualities can you apply to your own life?

Becoming My Own Greatest Hero

Becoming your own greatest hero is an uncomfortable idea for most people. Our culture doesn't make much space for heroes—or honor. We find ourselves *unworthy* to be a hero.

An unfortunate misunderstanding runs through some branches of Christianity about the meek being the good guys and the powerful being evil. In my reading, the Bible condemns self-importance, not self-esteem—love of money, not money—love of power, not power itself.

TODAY IN MY WORLD:

Do you instinctively feel worthy or unworthy to fill the shoes of a hero? Why?

Do you want a big breakthrough in your self-esteem—right now? If so, step boldly past your discomfort and declare yourself to be your own greatest hero.

Stand Tall, Breathe Deeply, Announce Boldly:
"I am Powerful. I am Worthy. I am a Hero."

How does it feel? Stay with the feeling and let it settle in. Keep breathing slowly and deeply. Visualize a heroic energy filling your body—rising from your feet, through your legs, your abdomen, your solar plexus, your chest and shoulders. Exhale your new power before it over-builds in your head. Keep breathing.

MAR Modeling my qualities on heroic beings is a lifelong practice. The models need not be human or even real. A participant in this process once listed a particular mountain as a hero. A character from a book can act as a model for me. Recognize the heroic in others and bring it to your own daily experience. I have done this in the following poem, which was prompted by my admiration for two amazing, heroic women: Sandra Grace, a kindred spirit and professional consultant, and Hillary Rodham Clinton. Under the harsh attentions of political scrutiny and continuous media spotlight, Clinton possesses a remarkable strength of purpose. She is unwavering in her commitment to a breadth of goals and ideals. A detractor of Clinton once said to me, "But she's so tough." I laughed and replied, "You say that as if it's a bad thing." This poem praises the tough.

This day I want to sing in praise of tough girls.

Tough girls deserve their own song, their own poem.
The girls that don't have hardened hearts, but they do have hardened skin. The ones that hit back when you hit them.
Hard. And they aim to hurt.
There's poetry in that. And justice, too.
I want to sing in praise of the tough girls.
The women who say, "Cry in your own towel, baby.
I've got troubles of my own."
We all do. We all have our own troubles. It's just
a matter of seeing them clearly. And walking them to
some other corner to sit. And then they give you a towel.
I want to write a poem for the women who can say,
"Get lost. Take it somewhere else:
I've already seen that show."
Grace has its place. Compassion prevails. And tough
girls make those things possible. They are the gatekeepers,
the door watchers, the ones who make it possible for the
girls who cry to write their poetry. They are the ones
who say, "Look, honey, look here. Even tough skin can
be temptingly beautiful. Even tough skin can be soft
when you know how to touch."
And it is.
I want to sing in praise of the tough women, the women

who do not apologize for the space they take on the planet.
Because these are the women, the riveters, the senators, these
are the women who make the road clear for me,
for all the rest of us. These are the women who clear spaces
for others to stand.
And they do.
I know these women cry. I know they do. I'm the
one who feels their tears. Their tears water a strong growing
plant, one that produces an aroma of fortitude for all the
world to take in and stand a little taller.
Today I sing the praises of the tough girls . . .
Today I'll borrow a little of their graces and see what
kind of plant we can grow together.

Tough girls? They are consummate self-nurturers. They
are certain that responsibility for their best practices lie
within them.

NURTURING MYSELF

JLH What do we need in order to be healthy and thrive? Freedom from stress and fear, healthy food in moderation, restful
sleep, physical movement, and play time. If we don't get ample
amounts of each of these, we are not much good to either ourselves or to those around us.

Far from it being selfish to nurture myself, it would be disre-
spectful both to myself and to those of my community for me
to do otherwise. To be of service to either myself or to those
around me, it is essential that I nurture myself.

Caring for oneself is very personal. My healthy glass of milk
might be your allergic reaction—my brisk walk might be your heart
attack. What follows are my opinions and what works for me.

Honoring my physical self is about what I call moderation and what Mary Anne calls balance.

Healthy Food in Moderation

Healthy eating is all about moderation. The first way in which moderation is important, is in having moderation about the level of concern we pay to our eating habits. If we pay no attention at all to our eating, we tend to grab whatever is handiest—the fast food, the chips—that doesn't work well.

Paying too much attention to our eating isn't a recipe for healthy eating either—or for a relaxed and joyful life. There is a potentially serious criticism of every food we might ever consider putting in our mouth. Relax, stop worrying, enjoy your food.

Moderation is also about variety. Generally, we eat healthier when we eat a wide variety of foods. While a diet of ice cream isn't ideal, neither is a diet of only tofu and seaweed. Perhaps your mommy taught you to eat your fresh vegetables—green, yellow, leafy—yes, your broccoli and your spinach—and every kind of squash you can find. And if she didn't teach you then, you can teach yourself now.

Moderation is about quantity—enough, as well as not too much. If you have a habit of overeating, there's always willpower, but the much easier and more enjoyable approach is to fill your life with so many other joyful activities and interests that over-eating ceases to dominate your life. Worry is a major cause of overeating, so use the rest of this book to transform your worries and suffering into joy.

Mostly, don't be overly concerned about food. What we are concerned about, we focus our attention on, and that drains our energy. Live joyfully, have many interests and activities, and your eating will usually take care of itself.

Sleep

Many of us experience troubled sleep—at least from time to time. Sometimes the cause is physiological. If our joints or muscles ache, or we have other pains, we are not going to sleep well, and we might consider a visit to our physician. Another cause of troubled sleep is worry, stress, and general emotional turmoil. For these, try the guided meditation that follows, the Inner Smile exercise in the Unity chapter, and the Release exercise in the Celebration chapter.

TODAY IN MY WORLD:
A GUIDED MEDITATION FOR RELEASING MYSELF TO SLEEP

Read this guided meditation into your voice recorder. When you are ready for sleep, darken the room, ensure that your bed coverings are light but comfortably warm, close your eyes, and play back the recording.

I sleep gently, with the light touch of Spirit upon my brow.

My dreams dance like angels around my head.

I sleep gently in the arms of Spirit.

As I inhale slowly and deeply, I visualize my body filling with purity and light.

As I exhale slowly and fully, I visualize each muscle relaxing.

With every exhalation, the relaxation moves down my body: forehead, face, jaw, neck, back, chest, arms, stomach, abdomen, hips, legs, feet.

I breathe in the pureness of relaxation and sleep.

I breathe out each and every trouble as I allow my worries to drain out my toes—my every exhale is a relaxation and release—I hold back nothing—I release every worry, every fear, every thought, every question, and every need to the grace of Spirit.

There is no need-ness, no should-ness, no wrong-ness.

I release my troubles, my concerns, my responsibilities.

There is nothing to do, there is nothing to say, there is
nothing—there is nothing to need, there is nothing to want.

I listen to the roar of the River of Life as it rushes from before
time toward forever.

I am timeless and placeless.

My shoulders sag and my neck turns to rubber as my every
muscle relaxes completely.

My breathing slows.

My every exhale becomes deeper.

My every in-breath becomes slower and shallower.

My every out-breath is a release—a short, sharp complete
voiding—I trust to release each and every molecule with
none held back.

I am oblivious to any sound or light.

I am in my own world of dark silence, undisturbed by the
world's twitching and murmuring.

There is nothing to do, there is nothing to say, there is nothing
to think—no should, no ought, no must—no might, no
could, no maybe.

I let the black is-ness overwhelm every thought, every
question, every doubt.

Movement

Movement is all about moderation and joy. My daily forty-minute
sunset walk on the beach is one of the happiest parts of my day.
The beach is a hundred feet below the level of the road, and by
the time I get back to the road, I'm sweating and breathing hard.
My walk takes me past a tasty snack of blackberries, great views of
seabirds, and occasionally sea otters and other water creatures.

Most days, the sunset inspires me to take its picture. My walk is relaxing and invigorating—hot days, cold days, or rainy days. Sometimes I listen to music on my mp3 player. Sometimes I record voice notes of the inspirations that often flow more freely on my walk than at my desk, sometimes I just listen to the sounds of nature. While different, each variation is magnificent.

Yoga and Qigong provide me gentle movement and stretching, as well as energetic and spiritual renewal. Dance is another form of movement that is fun and also healthful. Find forms of movement that are fun for *you*. This is choosing ways that honor your well-being.

MAR I've always preferred sitting and writing or reading to physical activity, but most recently I've taken walking into my routine. I began following *The Complete Guide to Walking*. Author Mark Fenton insists that a person of my level of fitness must begin with several weeks of twenty-minute walks. Ten out. Ten back. I'm suited up. I've got my mp3 player, and to the road I go. The music measures my steps. "Wide Open Spaces," "This Kiss," "100 Years," "We Built This City," and "Unwritten." The lyrics "the rest is still unwritten" inspire my steps.

The view is a perfect companion for a morning walk. I swing my arms long and walk in time with the music. The Olympic Mountains are a testimony to timelessness as I walk, wondering if this process will work over the long haul. Then I know it will work if I *do* the work. The next wondering comes . . . how much time will this add to the length of my life? That is truly unknowable because it can only be known by comparing two outcomes. I only get to play out one outcome. The real key comes in knowing that this exercise program adds attentiveness and energy, and therefore life and time, to my daily activities. These are the real and immediate benefits.

So I walk. The music plays, and I have completed one full circle in my community. There's a choice. Left turn for home or right turn to go around again? "Man, am I out of shape," I muse. With an ever-so-slight pause, the music is refraining the chorus of Five for Fighting's "100 Years," and I hear the phrase "there's never a wish better than this when you've only got 100 years to live." It feels like a personal health challenge from a music group I don't even know. Then, I glance up. Flying low and immediately above my head . . . two bald eagles. Let me be clear. They are not out over the water, not in over the trees. They are immediately over my starting-to-sweat head. Another challenge!

I hear the older comedian quoting, "If I had known I was going to live this long, I would have taken better care of myself." And with "100 Years" echoing in my mind, and the eagles still above me, I march around the development again. How would I deal with this previously undesired exercise routine if I knew I was going to live to one hundred? That's half again the years I've already lived. This time, with a small instruction manual, I could rock it.

I notice I've picked up my feet a little more. Just a little.

For the next bit I set down the wonderings and just enjoy the music. I enjoy seeing myself walking twenty minutes a day, no matter where I am or what I have to do for the coming two weeks.

On the stretch down an easy slope to the sanctuary I know as home, I feel invigorated. I feel fitness is possible, not a fantasy. I'm thinking in this routine I might become my own hero. And guess who comes close. Let me be clear: I mean *close*. A swoop over my head. I wave to my eagle friend, my soaring spirit messenger who comes and punctuates my walk with an exclamation point. There's the bald eagle immediately over me. A symbol of power and ability.

I make it home with the eagle and Natasha Bedingfield's assurance "the rest is still unwritten" supporting my hopefulness toward my own heroics.

Moderation—A Lifestyle Without Excess

JLH Extremes in lifestyle are advocated by some, with the best of intentions, but I prefer to be neither the couch potato nor the marathon runner. "Seek moderation in all things," is attributed to Aristotle, but essentially the same thing was said by ancient Taoists and by the Buddha, as well as by Benjamin Franklin and thoughtful sages of all cultures. An idea worth living.

One of the major themes in the life of the Buddha was his choice to adopt the Middle Way (moderation) in contrast to the wealth of his youth and the extreme self-denial with which he experimented. To honor yourself and your body, choose moderation.

Something Special—Just for Yourself

Between living lives of habit, and deeming ourselves unworthy of special consideration, we often don't think to take the best possible care of ourselves. Perhaps today is the day to try something new—just for *you*.

Often, that special consideration comes without cost—I'm worth a daily walk that renews my body and spirit. When doing something special for ourselves does have cost, it can be surprisingly low. For years, I bought the cheapest ballpoint pens. They wrote—and kept writing—most of the time. It was a functional choice. Then I discovered the smooth writing of better pens— the hand feel, the light pressure, the effortless flow, my sense of worthiness. No, I'm not talking about a two-hundred-dollar fountain pen. I'm talking about a two-dollar pen, in contrast to a fifty-cent pen. I'm worth it.

It's amazing what can make life flow much more easily. My wife and I bought an inexpensive second refrigerator. A lot more of an investment than a smooth writing pen but not exorbitant either. I was surprised by how much more smoothly the household started to flow. Easier meal planning—fewer trips to the grocery store. As with the pens, the refrigerator was a choice that vastly enhanced my enjoyment for a relatively small amount of money.

TODAY IN MY WORLD:

What relatively affordable small items have you been denying yourself because you don't feel worthy? What have you never even considered adding to your life? Be innovative.

Moderation in Exchange with Others

MAR My usual inquiry of the medical receptionist, "how ya doing?" as I checked into my doctor's office received a lengthy reply. She told me about the crazy pattern in the office all week, the unexpected sickness of not one but two souls for whom she was responsible, three grand annoyances the doctor had perpetrated upon her, and . . . the doctor was ready to see me before she could spout off the last few things.

This type of exchange reminds me of the classic comedy routine in which, in the supposed interest of immediacy, one comic piles so much in the arms of the other that physical comedy ensues. Walk into a wall, fall down. Imagine the possibilities. Art crosses over into real life with an excellent comedic line, "Need-to-know basis! You've told me more than I need to know." I use the word *balance*—balance in what I am willing to take in, consume, participate in. And balance in what I am willing to give out or share.

The image of a teeter-totter comes to my mind when I consider the process of balance in exchange. There's up, there's down, and that point of equal position between the two. Being all the way up might appear out of balance, but it's just part of the rhythm. The person on the apparatus is the best determiner of what is in balance and what is not. Talking about balance doesn't involve a precise formula as much as it involves indicators.

When you honor yourself, you know your own signs in relation to the teeter-totter of balance. Learn to recognize the warning beacons that you provide yourself when you are going out of balance. What are some of the signals that you transmit when becoming out of balance? Appetite shifts, crankiness, headaches? They are different for everyone. I have a measure that works consistently. I ask myself, "Am I drained or energized?" I am not asking if I am tired. I can be energized by something and still be weary. The mechanism is fundamentally mathematical: does something add or subtract, multiply or divide? I have an even better short-cut. *Enervate* means "to drain or weaken energy." *Innervate* means "to bring nerves to the body, to energize." When said aloud, they sound the same. I ask myself, "Which one is it for me with this _____" fill in the blank—person, entertainment, event, experience. Is this person speaking to me draining or energizing me? I answered that question when I good-naturedly stopped my doctor's receptionist from completing her tale of woe. I was kind in the manner that I did it—and I honored myself, my own nature, by avoiding the drain. This is a signal of my self-honor—that I am investing in an exchange, by choice, rather than accidentally pouring myself out. Or inappropriately absorbing or taking in. What are the indicators that you are honoring your true self? Have you been energized or drained?

Recently a radio interviewer asked me, "Isn't it kind of selfish to tend to your own needs first?" The answer was an immediate and emphatic "Absolutely not!" Honoring yourself is the most unselfish thing you can do. The first time I flew, I understood the ready metaphor in the flight attendant's instruction, "In the event of an emergency, an oxygen mask will drop down. Please place the mask on yourself first before assisting others." This is a familiar demonstration that we must fully care for ourselves before we can healthily serve others.

Honor of self is an excellent starting point in Simply an Inspired Life.

Chapter 4

FORGIVENESS—For Self and All

AFFIRMATION I Forgive Myself with Compassion—I forgive everyone, especially myself, for all actions and all inactions throughout my entire life. I accept that no one else has ever been to blame for either my joy or my suffering. The entire cause of all my joys and all my sufferings is my own emotional response to the events of my life, and I am committed to consistently distinguishing between my feelings about events and the physical occurrence of those events. I declare that everyone who has ever played any role in any of the events of my life is entirely without fault. ॐ

Would you rather be right or happy?
—A Course in Miracles

Don't take it personally—it's not usually about you.
—mar

Where there is no accusation of fault, there can be no anger.
—jlh

JLH I'm angry—they wronged me, they lied, they cheated. Why should I forgive them?

Forgiveness is not a reprieve that we give to someone else. Forgiveness for another's act or omission is a gift we give ourselves. We are the one who suffers the upset and the anger when we feel we have been wronged. It is our own blood pressure that rises when we hold on to resentment.

Forgiving others is a gift to yourself, given not because *they* deserve pardon, but because *you* deserve the serenity and joy that comes from releasing resentment and anger, and from embracing universal forgiveness.

WHO OR WHAT IS THERE TO FORGIVE?

"I forgive you." What is going on here? A lot of history always precedes those three words—some fact, and a lot of assumption. The person I'm forgiving did something—or at least I believe he did something. I believe what he did was wrong—that he was at fault—for doing what he did. In concluding that he was wrong, I applied a set of rules that I believe represent how things should be.

Having judged him guilty, I now offer to stay my vengeance by saying, "I forgive you."

For each of us, it's our rule book, we're the witness, prosecutor, judge, and jury, and then we get to say, "I forgive you," if we choose to. Although it seems as though we are dispensing punishment and then a reprieve to the perpetrator, we are actually condemning ourselves to suffering.

When I judge someone guilty, I inflict suffering upon myself. When I forgive him, I release my burden of suffering and give myself a gift of joy.

So what could be better than forgiveness? For all the remarkable power forgiveness has in healing our self-inflicted suffering, remember that there is never anything *to* forgive. How can there be nothing to forgive? The concept of forgiveness depends upon the idea that another person did something wrong. The idea of wrongness is based upon following, or not following, an arbitrary collection of rules. And who determines those rules? *That* is the crux of the matter. If you believe that you have the authority to dictate your own rules to the world, then breaching those rules becomes "wrong," and the concepts of vengeance and forgiveness gain a context, although a context without merit.

However, if you acknowledge that you don't have the authority to set the rules of the world, the sequence: rules defined, rules broken, vengeance or forgiveness, becomes meaningless from the outset because there is no agreed-upon set of rules. Based upon your own personal set of rules, you may believe that you have been wronged and hold the power of forgiveness, but remember that the other party acted according to their own set of rules. Believing that one's own rules hold supreme importance in the universe is an act of ego that is a sure cause of great suffering.

Perhaps next time we can just remain in joy by choosing not to judge others in the first place.

Open Mind, Open Hand

MAR Forgiveness lives in the present. It does not revisit the shrine of past offenses or borrow from the fear of the same old thing happening again. Forgiveness looks at the clock and understands that the time is now . . . and that is all there is. Forgiveness does not imply memory loss, it requires an open mind. Forgiveness requires the ability to see an event in the context of a new opportunity. Forgiveness also requires an open hand—a hand that is not holding on to the fibers of an old experience. An open hand is able to receive the lesson and move on. Forgiveness is willing to see a situation in the context of itself, rather than through a lens of being right or being wrong. Forgive does not exist alongside blame.

We hang on to our unhappiness or we don't. We are unhappy or we are not. We sit in silence and brood over all the things we have not done, or worse, all the things that others have not done. By contrast, we sit with music and muse on our dreams, the little slices that the day will give into the big pot of gold in the center of the table.

To you, dear reader, I would speak as if you are my friend, and say . . .

You aren't really asking me for forgiveness. You are asking yourself. I will be a mirror for you. You may forgive yourself, your long silences to your own soul, your long absences from your own priority party, your deft theft of all the things significant to the thriving nature of your days. I notice how quickly you trade your power for approval. Remember that such approval is transitory. It is dependent on the next thing you are willing to give up.

Giving up and giving away. Giving away is essential and, paradoxically, creates abundance. Giving up something—quid pro quo, trading this for that—is a taking, a robbery of the most insidious kind. It looks like a compromise, quiet kindness, sacrificial generosity, but in the harsh light of truth, giving up is equal to martyrdom. Harm to self. How can you tell the difference?

A real gift leaves your hand and gives you joy. You let it go and watch it have its own life. You don't own a bit of it anymore, because you gave it from fullness.

In giving up something, it leaves your hand and a stain remains behind. The stain reminds you what you had and no longer have. It reminds you to whom you handed it. You watch and see how the recipient uses it. You ask, "Do you still use that thing I gave you?" Because you gave it up instead of giving it away, you look for the trade back. You wait for the receiver to use it and express gratitude. You expect the receiver to give you something back that you wanted but hadn't the courage to specifically ask for or to acquire for yourself. That's not a gift. It's an undefined trade, a one-sided exchange with lots of room for disappointment, for rarely does the recipient understand the expectations attached to the gift.

I wonder about the gifts we give to ourselves. Do they get given with quid pro quo expectations too? If we do a specific task by Thursday we'll "gift" ourselves with an afternoon of quiet reading. That's not a gift. It's a trade. It's an incentive program to reward prescribed performance.

Forgive yourself. I say this to me as I say it to you.

Forgive yourself. Gift yourself with healing, certain welcome, the music that feeds your soul, the smells that soothe, the activity that gives back.

You are worthy. You deserve fine relationships just the way you are. Today, tell the truth as you know it. That's all you can do at any moment. You cannot speak or do more than you know. And here's the joy: you know everything you need to know.

Gift yourself and your friends with integrity, with forgiveness. Try these words, "I love you. Just you. All of you. The way and all the ways you are."

The Process of Forgiveness

I speak with people about the process of forgiveness and am amazed by two things: the diversity of the stories they tell, and the consistency of what people say about forgiveness. Most tell me that it means forgetting. Completely letting it go. Pretending, if you must, that the event never happened. Finding a place to stuff or set aside the hurt.

Some people tell me that there are some things they will never forgive, that they "won't give *them* the satisfaction" of forgiving them. Just recently I was talking with a professional associate about forgiveness. He said there were some things in his life that were unforgivable, that specifically, some actions a few folks had done were so awful, that he simply refused to forgive them.

After I listened to his stories I asked what he would think if I said that forgiveness had everything to do with him and nothing at all to do with the person who had committed the specific actions.

"What does forgiveness have to do with me?" he responded. "They're the ones who did this awful thing." He was earnest. It was more a rhetorical statement than a question.

"Look at yourself as a boat—a SAILboat, let's say—and there are these several incidents in your life that you insist you will not forgive. Picture this—each offense is a barge and its size depends on how much it hurt you. Each offense is attached to your sailboat by virtue of the fact that you will not forgive it. It is tied to you with a line. Your small sailboat not only has to move, under full sail, with all these barges attached to you, but it also has to navigate in a storm with these lines and weights. How much smoother would your SAIL be if you cut those barges loose?"

He asked me if that's how I managed my own hurts and forgiveness. I told him it was, that I first looked at the event as something that individual chose for him- or herself, then as a secondary effect it had something to do with me.

"No, I don't buy it. You mean to tell me that when somebody cheats on me, disrespects our bond, and violates our trust it's first about them?"

"Yes. It's an action taken from their own perspective and their own view on the world. The consequence it delivers to me is secondary." He was skeptical. I suggested, "Here's a rule of thumb: If I am able to see a thing as a weight on my SAIL, my life, it probably needs my forgiveness. And that forgiveness impacts me, first and foremost. I don't even need to speak the process out loud. Nope. No noble 'I forgive you' delivered with some level of drama. Forgiveness—it's all a process within me."

Our conversation went back and forth. I learned a second concern my associate had about forgiveness—that it would just open the door to allowing the same thing to happen to him all over again.

Somehow forgiveness has become confused with not learning a lesson or with not creating a new boundary. I can offer forgiveness and establish a boundary that means I do not involve that specific person in my life. I can forgive *and* remember.

I just saw my good friend burn his hand on a hot pan. He's been cooking all his life. He knows very well that a pan just removed from a recently hot stove top may burn him. He's had the experience. But he forgot. He neglected to observe all the information in his immediate experience. My doctor friend has the same concern about some larger issues in his life. He's afraid that if he forgives, he is also required to forget how he was hurt, and he will again be injured in precisely the same way.

Surely it is much more generous to forgive and remember, than to forgive and forget.
—Maria Edgeworth (1767–1849) Irish writer

Forgiving allows us to cut the line on the weight of a hurt, and remembering allows us to perceive potential patterns and begin the process of creating a new, more joyful way.

EMBRACING MY PAST

JLH The events of the past cannot be altered. Whether our father said the words "you are a bad boy" when we were six, or a classmate pulled our hair, or we got pregnant at sixteen, or we cut our mother's throat with a kitchen knife, none of that can be changed now. Like everyone else at every other moment of history, we did the best we could at each instant. We can't go back and replay our actions.

You are shocked at the part about the kitchen knife? I am happy if that doesn't happen to be your dirty little secret, but every one of us has dirty little secrets of which we are deeply ashamed and that cause us immense ongoing suffering throughout our lives. Our level of suffering has relatively little to do with how society ranks the severity of our secret, and everything to do with our own degree of shame. Usually, we cannot atone for these secrets, and when we can, it often provides little relief from our shame and suffering.

Throat-cutting may not be common, but other lifelong traumas are remarkably common. The U.S. government agency Centers for Disease Control and Prevention quotes a survey in which

10% of women and 2% of men "reported experiencing forced sex at some time in their lives." Many other studies include other forms of sexual abuse, such as fondling, and adjust for victims' tendency to under-report abuse. They suggest a prevalence of sexual abuse in the United States more than double the government statistics. Regardless of the exact numbers, every such incident traumatizes two lives. The victim faces a lifetime of shame, while the abuser, who in most cases was also abused as a child, continues to feel unending shame and guilt.

Childhood bullying is another cause of lifetime trauma for both parties. A 2001 publication of the U.S. Department of Education found "14 percent of students ages 12 through 18 reported that they had been bullied at school." As with sexual abuse, the lives of both the victim and the perpetrator of bullying are contaminated by shame—the aggressor for having injured a fellow human, and the exploited for their self-perceived failure in having been unable to defend themselves.

This book is not about sexual abuse, bullying, or any other specific cause of suffering—it is about easing all our emotional suffering. Suffering is suffering—the original cause and whether we were the victim or the perpetrator aren't especially relevant in our quest to relieve the suffering.

You may be shocked and outraged when I say that it doesn't matter whether we were the victim or the perpetrator. From the point of view of justice in society, of course it matters, but from the point of view of joy and suffering, it doesn't. Even if the victim could extract vengeance on the perpetrator, that would only bring him more suffering—never joy.

As *A Course in Miracles* asks, "Would you rather be right or happy?" If you want to be right, focus on the distinction between victim and perpetrator. If you want to be happy, focus on the fact that we are all just fallible, suffering human beings—each doing the best we can.

Everyone has their own little secrets that cast a pall over their lives, and secrets greatly impact all their interactions. If a husband was abused as a child, he will never be as open and trusting of his wife as he otherwise would be. If a wife was belittled and deprived of love and nurture as a child, or abused in a prior adult relationship, she will tend to view her husband through jealous, envious, and needy eyes. Their spouses don't deserve that suspicion and desperation; it is transferred onto them from their relationship with their parents, prior lovers, and others. And the suffering continues. But if the abused husband and the neglected wife are able to forgive their past injustices, however grave, they can be free to experience joy in their current relationships.

Forgiving My Past

MAR I allow myself the freedom of vulnerability to all that is good. I am open, with joy, to all which is a balm to me. I wrap myself in clothes of safety, of understanding, of intention. I rest in the light of forgiveness. I forgive myself and others for that which is done (and better left undone) and also for that which is not done (and better if done!). I give myself permission to enjoy this moment without analysis. I freely release any uncertainty, regret, fear. I hold tenderly those I love. Compassionately, I touch those I have hurt—or who have hurt me. I sing of my singularity and bask in the emanation of all I am and may be. This life is not an isolated experience but one of mutuality. In understanding this—the adventure begins.

If you haven't forgiven yourself something, how can you forgive others?

—Delores Huerta

When I embrace a friend, it generally implies welcome. It can also express acceptance or comfort. When I embrace my friend—I always let her go. I do not embrace and continue the embrace. Embrace implies an action . . . and that the action stops. So it is with the process of embracing my past.

I welcome my past. I acknowledge its presence and impact. I express my affection and gratitude. My past is the vehicle that brought me to this moment. I am grateful for the ride. I am here now. Then I let it go. The past brought me, but it need not keep me in this place. To forgive my past means at some point I let it go.

There is a significant difference between understanding your past and using your past as an excuse. I was involved in a surprise party which went awry when I was five years old. It's predictable, isn't it, that I might tell you I am still not fond of surprise parties? That experience is a vehicle which brought me to where I am. I can accept that, embrace it as part of what makes me unique. I can choose to view surprise parties differently from the way I have since I was five, or I can continue to be guided in my choices by my experience.

You'll recognize the phrase, "That was then, this is now." With this phrase in mind, I can forgive the experience. That particular surprise party did not go well, but not all will go that way. I can recognize that cutting the line to the past enables me to move forward from where I am right now. And I may experience a surprise party that I like.

Don't let a past you can't change write your future script.

—Dr. Morris Massey

My history can quietly determine my ways, but once I recognize this is happening, I can change my ways. There's the significant key—recognizing it. How do I embrace and forgive past events when I don't actively recognize them as historical components that influence my decisions constantly?

As a young woman, I railed against my history. I made sweeping assessments such as if I ever had a family I would raise my children differently than my parents raised me. I wouldn't make the same mistakes I saw my brothers make raising their children. And yet I allowed my history to determine the direction and content of my days. It literally filled my sails and steered the ship of my life all kinds of ways. And in those days, I just basically did my best to hang on and not get tossed into the sea. I did not recognize the patterns and the things I learned from my environment without even noticing.

I know you have these moments in your life. The moments you can count on your fingers which contribute to that profound shift in your perspective, when your life changes, forever. Rarely do they receive the respect they deserve as they are happening. It is in looking back that we are able to identify the moment our road changed direction or, even more than that, transformed.

Here's one such moment. I had countless hours of lost time on the time clock at my job. The Alzheimer care facility housing my father seemed to be in continual crisis and need. Furthermore, I appeared to be on the top of the call list of my wide circle of friends who frequently called for assistance.

I was called into a meeting by my boss S. and coworker G., and it became clear to me that I was being chastised, at best. S. asked, for the second time, why I'd had to leave work early the day before.

"Why?" I responded. Her question puzzled me. I had recounted the situation once already, and she had been at work the previous day when everything happened. She knew all about my friend's troubles at home, her boyfriend, the kids, the car, the immediate need for a ride.

"I told you yesterday. I am very upset . . ." and I launched, again, into the complete details of the most recent calamity.

When I finished, G. asked, "What does that have to do with you?"

Has she taken periodic leave of her senses? I wondered. "What do you mean?"

"What does Barbara's experience of yesterday have to do with you having to leave your job and you being upset right now?"

Patiently, I started explaining the nature of Barbara's relationship with this abusive individual, how often she turned to me for comfort, support, and often, to pitch her out of some difficult game she was in.

G. interrupted in the midst of the narrative and spent some time explaining the concept of living in the present moment, addressing the significance of *now* as opposed to yesterday or tomorrow or even five minutes ago. All the while, S. was supportively listening and nodding her head.

The words that filled her paragraphs after her reference to the now have wandered into the file room of my memory's library. Far in the back. But I remember how she ended her speech: "You have nowhere you *have* to go. You have nowhere you *must* be . . . except right where you are. Now." Maybe she expressed that in the now dwells perfect balance. Perhaps she used the metaphor of how dipping our toes in the sea of the past or the river of the future takes us out of balance. It's something she would have said.

I remember feeling as if I had been chastised for doing something very wrong and yet not understanding what was so wrong. I was just trying to help a friend. It exceeded my life experience and my perspective of the moment to grasp the enormity and simplicity of G.'s message. "Is this because of my having to leave early yesterday? Am I in trouble for—"

"Sugar, if this was simply about you leaving early yesterday, or coming late, or having to take extra time at lunch, you would have lost your job a long time ago. This is about you. We care for you. I see such special things in you, and yet your life is filled with everyone else's troubles, *plus* your own. I've found in my own life that managing to deal with my own trouble takes time enough without adopting everybody else's."

I was still stuck on the whole not having anywhere else to be. I had so many other places I had to be. In fact, I always seemed to be in a hurry to get somewhere other than where I was.

S. had predicted the difficulty these concepts would present. I had spent the bulk of my young life tending the challenges in the lives around me. She had brought along a book she hoped would make more sense to me. *How to Live in the World and Still Be Happy.* Hugh Prather was the author. I left for lunch confused. Before I returned to work the following day, I had read that book at least four times. It was marked, starred, underlined, and some of the pages were stained by my tears. I was no longer so confused.

Hugh Prather's life experience intersected with my life experience and changed the way I would sail through the rest of my days. Did I become a new person? Did I experience an utter and complete and immediate transformation? Did I offer myself total forgiveness once and for all? Yes. And no. The transformation was immediate in that I looked at my past differently—and never saw it the same way again. I embraced where I had come from and recognized that what I once saw as shortcomings and inhibitors could instead be springboards. My history would no longer write my future.

As to the transformation, it continues. To this day I remember the power of the now . . . the extraordinary compassion and forgiveness that are present when I am present to the immediacy of my life as it is right now—not with an offense that occurred a while ago or with a sadness that shadowed my days when I was five. Or eleven. Or thirteen.

Those moments . . . those profound shifts which inexplicably change the character of our lives. What are yours? Isn't it interesting how many of them seemed almost ordinary at the moment? It was something as ordinary as a lunch and the gift of a book.

TODAY IN MY WORLD:

Identify some of those moments in your own past which significantly changed you. Consider them as if they were literal teachers or instructors. Embrace them. Thank them. Ask yourself if there is reason to consider forgiveness.

Coming to terms with the past—embracing it as a teacher, expressing gratitude for its assistance in becoming the person you are in this moment—provides momentum to the dynamic process of forgiveness.

An Autobiographical Scrapbook

JLH An autobiographical scrapbook is a fairly large project, but it is a remarkably powerful tool in facing and overcoming childhood issues and reaching forgiveness. The first time I made one, my insights were nothing short of amazing.

One of the techniques that added to the power of documenting my childhood was writing about each year in the way a child of that age would speak. Thus, on my four-year-old page, the words are "Mommy, I'm afraid of strangers," rather than some adult psychology about fear. Through the process, I learned the age and circumstances at which my painful habits and fears first appeared, and I gained tremendous insight into my history, my sufferings, and my nature.

TODAY IN MY WORLD:

Make an autobiographical scrapbook with at least one page for each year of your life. Use photos or drawings along with a little text. Focus on major events, but include something for each year, even if you don't have any photos for the year and your memory is vague. Use the major events of each year as a structure for recalling your feelings—your fears, your resentments, your regrets, and your disappointments, as well as your accomplishments, hopes, dreams, and joys. Note especially when your feelings changed from the previous year. If you feel that you are ugly, not smart enough, not likeable, or such, pay attention to when you first became aware of that self-judgment and what major events immediately preceded its appearance. The process may amaze you.

Freedom from My Past—Choosing a Joyful Life

Here is a recipe for unchaining yourself from the suffering of your past, and for gaining immense freedom, comfort, and joy:

1. Acknowledge that who you were in the past is not the person you are today. Your past self did the very best that you could, given the knowledge, emotions, and prior experience that you had to draw upon at the time.

2. Create a new and more loving story to explain each event in your autobiographical scrapbook. The event, "A classmate pulled my hair," may have carried the

emotionally charged story: "My best friend Jane turned on me and pulled my hair right in front of the whole class. I was so embarrassed and angry that I cried and didn't speak to Jane for the rest of the year. How could she do that to her best friend?"

A more loving story would be: "Jane was desperately seeking the attention and approval of her classmates and latched upon the idea of pulling my hair to get a laugh. She was completely focused on herself and her own perceived need for attention. It wasn't about me."

Remember that neither story is what a video camera would have recorded, so neither story is more accurate than the other. The difference is that one version causes suffering, while the other brings inner peace. Choose inner peace.

3. Forgive every wrong you think was ever inflicted upon you. Forgive for your own sake, so you may release the venom—the anger and resentment within yourself—and regain your joy and serenity. Have compassion for everyone who has ever been a player upon the stage of your life.

4. Forgive yourself completely. Forgive yourself for having created a story of suffering. Forgive all the angers, resentments, jealousies, and all the other emotions of suffering. Have unbounded compassion for yourself at all times and under all circumstances.

5. Give thanks for everything that has occurred to bring you to this moment. Every event that has ever occurred has played a crucial role in who you are today.

The story from above might continue: "If Jane hadn't pulled my hair, I wouldn't have felt the need to compensate by proving that I was a better student, and I might not have received an A in science, studied biology, gone to UCLA, met Tom in anatomy class, and . . . So my beautiful daughter Amy is a direct result of Jane pulling my hair in fourth grade."

RECURRING PATTERNS—UN-LEARNING AND RE-TRAINING

As children, we learn the rules of the world. More specifically, we learn the rules of the adults who control our world. We are excellent learners, and our adults are accomplished trainers who are adept in the use of both punishment and reward. It has been like this from the dawn of time, and will continue for as long as humans survive.

While that sounds depressing at best, much of what we are taught as children is essential to our survival. Adults teach us early and firmly not to wander into traffic, not to eat toadstools, and not to imitate birds when we reach the edge of a cliff.

Adults also teach children to believe certain things about themselves—both positive and negative. These teachings may be a direct and cruel, "You're fat. Don't eat so much," or a subtle and well-intended, "Your sister is so thin and beautiful."

We may have been taught that we are fat, stupid, and lazy— or smart, handsome, and gifted. Surprisingly, either childhood message has a negative impact on our adult lives.

An acquaintance of mine complained that her mother had ruined her life by consistently expressing unconditional love and praise, sending her to the best schools, buying her almost anything she wanted, and expressing confidence that she would grow up to be a beautiful, successful, confident woman. It may sound as if my friend received an ideal childhood training, but *she* didn't think so. Her complaint was that by making her child-hood so idyllic, her mother had failed to prepare her for the miseries of adulthood.

The bottom line is that our parents and the other adults in our young life did the best they could given the nature of being human and the trainings that they themselves received as children. As a parent or other adult trainer of children, we will also do an absolutely miserable job of child training (at least in the eyes of our children), and we will also do the very best we can given the nature of being human and the various trainings we received as children.

Breaking the Recurring Patterns

Here are three ways in which we can take action to break the recurring patterns that originated in our childhood trainings:

1. Forgive our parents and adult trainers for *everything* they ever did or didn't do.
2. Forgive ourselves for *everything* we have ever done or not done.
3. Un-learn whatever childhood trainings we received that are not serving us well today, and re-train ourselves in ways that serve us better and create more satisfaction and joy in our life.

Our major tools for un-learning and re-training are astute observation and questions. There is a reason for everything we do and, except when we are specifically conscious of another explanation, the reason is because we were trained that way as children.

In the Choice chapter, we will ask ourselves many questions about why we do what we do, but for now, simply focus on re-training yourself to see joy in all of life.

OWNING MY SHADOWS WITH COMPASSION

We would never be conscious of joy if there were no suffering.

—jlh

Emotional states come in matched pairs such as happy and sad, loving and hateful—an inspiring emotion and a matching emotion of suffering that we term a *shadow* emotion. Without the contrast of a shadow emotion, we would never experience the joy of an inspiring emotion.

We have all experienced shadow emotions, and we will continue to—they are an inescapable part of life. The best we can do is to consciously accept our shadows and forgive ourselves for them.

Anger is one of the shadow emotions that most clouds our lives. Along with blame and fault, anger occurs in the fourth stage of the Cycle of Self-Inflicted Suffering, following the disappointment stage.

We are always angry *at* someone, or angry *about* something that someone did. Even when we just say, "I am angry," the *at* or *about* is always implied. It is human nature to associate upsetting circumstances with being someone's fault—to want to blame someone, even if we are the someone to be blamed. This association of event with fault is the nature of anger. Imagine hearing, "I am feeling angry just because I am feeling angry today. No specific action or event is the cause of my anger, and neither I nor anyone else is at fault." Hmmm ... that's just not the nature of anger. We simply cannot feel anger unless we identify someone at whom to direct it—someone to blame. Forgive yourself for your anger.

Neediness

A feeling of gratitude is an inspiring emotion, while its shadow—neediness—causes us great suffering.

Neediness comes from envy and jealousy, which come from either having less than yesterday, or from having less than one's neighbor.

—jlh

When I was quite young, one of my mother's favorite expressions was, "Comparisons are odious." It turns out that this saying dates back to 1440 or before—definitely a well-established observation. Why are comparisons odious, disgusting, repulsive? They cause envy and jealousy.

In concept, it's straightforward to overcome our sense that we don't have enough if we have less of something than our neighbor has. Concept is one thing—human instincts are another.

Rationally, we are far better off to have five loaves when our neighbor has twenty than to have two loaves when our neighbor has only one. But instinctively, it's the other way around—as numerous psychological studies confirm. What to do?

In this, as in all cases where our instincts and painful childhoods cause us suffering, the only real answer is compassion. This is a time to have compassion for ourselves, and for everyone else whose instinct drives them to envy and jealousy—which means everyone, to some extent. This is a time to love ourselves, and to speak gently to ourselves as we remind ourselves of our abundance.

MAR A pendulum swings. In physics it is frequently quoted that every action has an equal and opposite reaction. Indeed there's no *this* without *that*. And certainly there is no light without dark. A light casts its own shadow, doesn't it?

Right out of our news reports and history books . . . the advocate for children's rights abuses his own children, the router of corruption fills his own closet with corrupt actions, the loudest opponent of drug assistance programs is addicted to prescription painkillers.

These are their shadows. We all have them. Christina Baldwin, in *Life's Companion,* said, "Forgiveness is the act of admitting we are like other people."

People tell me I am the model of inspiration.
It is because I know the depth of despair.

People tell me I draw out their deepest thoughts and express their most intimate feelings as if I have known them all my life—
It is because I know profound isolation and understand the remarkable place of separation.

People tell me I am wise and patient—
I have made so many decisions that were unwise and my hot temper has curtailed conversation, created rough waters, and harmed relationships.

When I work with inmates, I ask them to identify their shadow selves. To make a list of those strengths and skills they demonstrated to commit the act that landed them in prison.

They do. It's inevitably a very dismal list. Later I asked them to create a different list. A list of their strengths. Their most noble, highest qualities. The things that people who love them and support them tell them ("Hey man, you are really good at that . . .").

Then we draw lines. From shadow to strength. I ask them to connect the opposites, the thing that is most *unlike* the other. And I'll tell you what—almost item per item, they match up. The shadows always lead to the strengths when you follow the line.

Interestingly, people are often more familiar with their shadows than they are with their strengths.

It can be an uncomfortable experience operating within your shadow. Coming to accept the shadow as the balance point on the spectrum of our strengths creates a different view and provides a path to forgiveness of ourselves and owning our shadows.

Forgiveness has been explored by skeptics and scholars for thousands of years. Formulas have been applied to forgive-ness—such as "seven times seventy." In Matthew 18:22 in the New Testament, Jesus was asked how many times someone should be forgiven. Seven? He answered, "Not just seven, but seventy." This is not to say that we should count the number of times we offer forgiveness, but rather that we should draw on a large resource of forgiveness.

Once you have completed the strength/shadow exercise practice, remind yourself to have an open mind/open hand. Hold an open hand in front of you. An open hand is unable to hold on to anything: it is ready for a gift. The gift of forgiveness. Ask yourself what gift you might be ready to receive in your open hand.

Chapter 5
GRATITUDE—In Everything

AFFIRMATION I Receive All of Life with Thanksgiving—I have gratitude for *everything* that has ever occurred to bring me to this moment. I give thanks for the joys and the sufferings, the moments of peace and the flashes of anger, the compassion and the indifference, the roar of my courage and the cold sweat of my fear. I accept gratefully the entirety of my past and my present life. ৵

We must let go of the life we have planned, so as to accept the one that is waiting for us.
—Joseph Campbell

Gratitude is the light in the dark corners of each day.
—mar

My life is a miracle. I give thanks that I'm me.
—jlh

JLH I welcome Life into my home as an honored guest. Life arrives at my door looking tired from the journey, a little mud splattered, and burdened with the baggage of long travels. Still, her elegance is unmistakable, and I recognize her as my most honored guest.

As I install Life in my back bedroom, I sort through her baggage. Some clothing is soiled, some is torn, some has been outgrown and doesn't fit anymore—that is how long Life has been on the road. Opening her other bags, I find new clothes that have never been worn—a party dress for which the appropriate celebration has not yet occurred, swaddling clothes for infants yet unborn, a walking stick for someone not yet crippled, and a mourning dress for one still quite alive.

Life is quite the guest. She certainly has her moments. At times, she sweeps cheerfully through my house with the grace of a ballerina and the voice of a nightingale—other times, she lurches from room to room littering my home with her cast-offs. On occasion, she engages me in a brilliant philosophical conversation so enthralling that I think I am debating Socrates.

Life is a bit eccentric and can never quite seem to appear fully put together. Sometimes she dresses for the ball, but her lipstick is smudged—sometimes she digs in my garden while wearing high heels—often she wears her favorite purple dress and red hat regardless of the occasion.

Whenever I look at my honored guest, I see the face of God. However crotchety or out-of-sorts, however elegant or engaging, however she surprises me on this particular day, Life is always my most honored guest, and I am thankful she stopped by for a visit.

LIVING THE UNCONCERNED LIFE

Unconcerned doesn't sound so great at first. In suggesting that we should be living the unconcerned life, I may seem to be advocating living unconsciously—without attention, thought, or compassion. Shouldn't we want to be concerned about the affairs of our lives and show concern for the welfare of others? While being concerned might indicate that we are interested, have caring feelings, and consider something or someone important, at the bottom line, being concerned is being worried, and worry is just a nagging form of fear.

Living the unconcerned life is living a life without anxiety or worry—especially in those situations where anxiety and worry would seem to be expected and natural.

Recently, the stock market saw its greatest drop in thirty years, and my own stocks—the source of my retirement—fell even faster than the broad market. It would be expected and natural for me to be concerned. Was I concerned? Yes. My tight chest and shallow breathing don't lie. Concerned and afraid.

So what's all this about living the unconcerned life, if I have concerns? It's a matter of degree and consciousness. How long and how intensely do I remain concerned? How quickly am I able to regain conscious control over my level of concern? How quickly can I return to expressing my gratitude for all of life?

Most of us are concerned about money—to some degree and in some way. The majority of us think we don't have enough. A few of us think that money is bad or evil and believe that no one should be allowed to be wealthy. This is equally an intense concern about money.

Whatever our beliefs, fears, desires, jealousies, and other emotions regarding money, our concern is measured by the amount of time and the level of intensity we direct toward the subject of money. To be unconcerned about money is to spend no time or energy whatsoever on the subject.

Money is just one example of our concerns. Whatever we direct our time and energy toward that doesn't give us joy is a concern.

What if I just pretended everything was easy?
—mar

TODAY IN MY WORLD:

How much time and energy do you spend on what you wear? What if clothes were merely something to keep you warm? Which aspects of personal grooming give you joy, and which are burdens that you endure out of a fearful need for approval? How much time and energy do you spend on your concerns about how you look, whether you are liked and respected, what you eat, your health, your bank account, your job, your retirement, your family, your safety, the weather, prices, shortages, government, big business, terrorists, crime, epidemics, foreign affairs, the economy, and everything on the eleven o'clock news?

Concern is about the time, energy, and emotion we direct toward something or someone—not whether we are for something or against it. If I spend time and energy proselytizing that fancy clothes are frivolous, I am fully as concerned about wardrobe as if I dutifully direct that time and energy toward making my own costume acceptable to others.

Concern is a natural emotion for humans, but we can minimize our suffering by recognizing the nature of our concerns, and by consciously focusing our attention on our gratitude for the joys of our life.

GRATITUDE FOR ALL PEOPLE AND FOR ALL OF LIFE

Why would we want to be grateful for *all* of life? Wouldn't being grateful for all of life imply being grateful for war, starvation, sickness, poverty, death, suffering?

Theological history is filled with discussion over the apparent contradiction between belief in an all-powerful loving God and the obvious suffering in the world. The argument goes something like this, "How could an all-powerful loving God either create suffering ("evil" to theists) or just sit back and watch without doing anything to help?"

> *How could anyone believe in a benevolent and omnipotent God after this?*
>
> —Voltaire [said in response to a 1755 earthquake in Lisbon during the All Saints' Day celebration in which 15,000 people died—mostly in churches filled to capacity.]

My personal theological response would be: "Who are we to know the mind of God? In the words of Alexander Pope, 'Whatever is, is right.' Obviously a loving omnipotent God is a better judge of what is best for us than we are." But this book isn't about theology, it's about living a joyful life.

> *Our gratitude for all people and all of life is a gift to ourselves that grants us joy and spares us suffering.*
> —jlh

When we express gratitude, we become joyful—when we are resentful, we suffer. It's a choice. My conscious choices are always for joy.

What Is Love?

When we feel that warm, embracing, timeless, placeless, egoless, unbounded connection with all of creation, we are experiencing unconditional love. When we feel bonded with our community or our nation, we are experiencing neighborly or patriotic love. When we feel bonded with our family and friends, we are experiencing familial love. When our hormones go *bong,* we are experiencing romantic love. When we admire, respect, and honor ourselves, we are experiencing self-love.

Is one kind of love better than another? Comparisons may be odious, but more fundamentally, the several kinds of love are barely even related. In many languages, these differing concepts do not even share the same word. It's like *hot* (high temperature) and *hot* (spicy)—there is a slight, but only slight, relationship between the concepts. In Spanish, there is no confusion between caliente and picante.

Have gratitude for all forms of love.

Gratitude for Community, Family, Loved Ones

Cooperative behavior is a fundamental basis for the success of the human species. Group living works best for us. Give thanks for our neighbor—the farmer, the grocer, the teacher, the fireman, the friendly hand when we're sick or grieving.

Before cars, airplanes, telephones, and the Internet, people could only gain a sense of community and belonging by interacting with their immediate neighbors. That concept only works well for small neighborhoods—up to about one hundred fifty people. After that, groups tend to become anonymous and cease to have a community feel. Today, most of us need to look beyond our physically closest neighbors to find our community. One of the best things that religious groups do is provide community for their members. Give thanks for our professional communities, our social communities, our political communities, our religious communities, even our online communities.

What does it mean to be family? Our ancestors are family. Our blood relatives are family. Those we share a home with are family. Whenever we share a close enough bond with someone to call them family, blood brother, or sworn friend, they too become family. Have gratitude for your entire family.

Our sons and daughters are always our children—whether they are newborn or they have their own children. Always have gratitude for your children—especially when they wake you at three A.M. because they can't sleep.

Some of us have relationships with our blood relatives that are uncertain at best, but that doesn't mean that we can't enjoy a loving family. The most wonderful family is the one we choose—whether we happen to share blood with them or not. Have deep gratitude for your chosen family.

Our loved ones—whether by blood, by marriage, or by choice—are delicate treasures. If we hold them too close, they break—as a butterfly would. By honoring and enjoying the freedom of our loved ones, we gain our own freedom. Have the courage to trust that the beautiful butterflies of your life will return—or not—as life intends.

What is a friend? There are many aspects to friendship. To the cynical, my friend is the enemy of my enemy. To the insecure, my friend is someone who shares my points of view. A friend is usually someone I like and someone I feel comfortable talking things over with. A true friend is someone whom I am grateful to have in my life. Have gratitude for your friends.

Gratitude for Our Animal Companions

Pets have a special place in millions of homes. If there are animal companions in your life, have gratitude for them. Have gratitude for every woof, meow, and accidental puddle.

> **TODAY IN MY WORLD:**
>
> Consider writing a story of gratitude about the people, places, and creatures in your life. It would be, essentially, a short biography of how your gratitude plays a significant role in your life. I will share an example that will both demonstrate the process and, I hope, help you remember some forgotten gratitudes of your life. I wrote this as I learned my sweet Labrador retriever only had a few days left to live. Expressing my gratitude in this way is also a way to embrace and face grief.

MAR   LITTLE ANGEL DOG

Mister Judah ben-Gurion Longfellow Radmacher Hamilton

I'd expressed my interest in a lab puppy but decided the time was not right for a puppy. Months later, an unexpected call came from Longfellow Kennels on a hot August afternoon.

"I know you said your life right now didn't have room for a dog, Mary Anne," began this phone call.

"I've never seen a little guy work so hard to get back to a place. We've placed this puppy with three different families and for reasons, none of which had anything to do with him, he's landed back here with us. We think he belongs with you. We would like to send him home with you as a gift."

Two hours later I'd assembled a kennel, bowls, bed, leash, collar, food, and five friends. We stood and watched the pups frolic in the grass half an acre away.

A black head popped up. We all stood in a line—and that little boy dog came running. Straight into my arms he jumped, and I swear I heard so clearly, "So, this is what home looks like. What took you so long?"

Judah started melting the winter of my heart. He began teaching me to say the words, "I love you," more easily and more generously. He started helping me think more largely beyond my circumstances.

Training. Stories. Parties and a dog that got slipped treats and loved balloons and ice cream. That dog was adored by everyone who met him. Judah, given a name of a warrior who was wise and led by strength and softness. A dog with a Jewish philosophical bent.

I was grateful this dog loved to travel and liked to be anywhere I was. A dog who saw and protected me from people who intended me harm. He walked along the water's edge but did not like the cold of water too much. A Labrador who didn't seem to like to swim. Go figure.

This dog raised me the finest way into my best years of adulthood just like my last black Labrador who raised me as a child in the backyard of my youth.

. . .

A business closed. A career shifted. Judah grew large. A marriage came. More travel than ever. A move to a no-dogs-allowed place. I sought a better opportunity for Judah and his dieting dogness. The family that said they would care for him in the event of my untimely death had a family conference which yielded an unreserved, "Yes." The dog who loved to travel flew for the first time in his life to the household of my closest friends.

Everything I saw in his life in Illinois filled me with joy.
I was happy to visit and see my words and photo still
had a place of honor on the family refrigerator—which
was filled from top to bottom with important ephemera.
I saw Judah on a great path to fitness, he was running
with the big dogs, happily swimming around in rivers,
and loving his new family. I was most grateful that
he remembered and welcomed me. In fact, he almost
knocked me over with his unrestrained greeting.

. . .

The first winter came with a chronic cough. Vet visits.
Medication. Tests. Is it this? No. Is it this? No. Let's take
an x-ray. Looks like cancer. Could it be . . . anything
else? Probably not.

. . .

As Judah's health declined, I hired a dog whisperer
to help us in our grief. She tells us that he does not
think he has long to live . . . and isn't too interested in
experiencing large levels of pain.

She says that he loves his people. All of them. He
wants to be sure he's done a good job with the kids. He
would like one last balloon party and some vanilla ice
cream. He mentioned he wouldn't mind having a bit
more fat in his diet.

The dog whisperer asked if there was anything
I wanted to tell Judah. I wanted him to know how
grateful I was for him being the best teacher of my life.
The dog whisperer told me Judah had learned something
important from me. What? Perseverance. Also, he
wanted me to know that there was still something I
needed to work on.

"What is that, Judah?"

"You need to laugh more. You are too serious."

Judah shared other observations for the rest of the family and couldn't resist putting in a plug for comfort in his final days: he wanted a softer bed and he would appreciate if the dad's music was played more often than the sixteen-year-old's music. Judah made it clear he wasn't sure how long he could hang on and asked if I could please come to visit in Illinois in the next two weeks. Kim asked, "What do you want, Judah?

After he thought awhile he said he only wanted two things: me to come visit and to be on the refrigerator, too. Three days after my last visit Judah went on to the next place where little angel dogs get to go.

As I flew away from Illinois I whispered, "You'll always be on my refrigerator door, Mister Judah-Buddha. You will have the high place in my heart as my finest teacher. Maybe I taught you a little about perseverance, but you taught me how to thaw my heart and give my love unconditionally. Everyone who knows and loves me now, knows for well and certain, that if they are grateful for who I am, they have to also be thankful for you, little angel dog."

My teacher continued providing me lessons, even from states away, and even as he prepared to leave the planet. I am so grateful that you worked diligently to come to a place at my side, and in the hearts of your new family, so that we could all see what it is that home looks like.

Gratitude for the Flow of Life

JLH Visualize yourself standing at the mouth of the mighty Mississippi River, shouting, "Stop! Reverse course. Please flow upstream today." See yourself on the beach at Key West commanding a giant hurricane to just calm down and stop being such a blowhard. Even imagine instructing your cat, "Bark." Unless you have a Moses complex, you are not going to take any of these suggestions seriously.

In our own lives, though, we make equally unreasonable demands of the universe on a daily basis. We try to push the river and wonder why it doesn't start flowing upstream.

Observe the flow of the River of Life. Allow the River of Life to flow past without judgment. Give thanks for the River of Life— for its every meander, its every twist and surge, its power, and its certain uncertainty.

Gratitude for Rainbows and Butterflies

Our rainbows and butterflies are the small miracles of our life— little things that are so easy to overlook, yet awe inspiring when we take a moment to notice and to pay attention. Give thanks for the rainbows, for the butterflies, for the bright blue sky and the soft fog, for the tree veiled in the season's first frost, for the baby's laugh, for the touch of a hand and the whispered "I love you."

Gratitude for the Bounty of the Earth

There is something magical about a Thanksgiving cornucopia overflowing with the fruit of the earth—the winter squashes, the corn, the apples.

TODAY IN MY WORLD:

Select one small fruit—a grape or a slice of apple. Take your fruit to a grassy area. Sit comfortably on the ground—with your back to a tree if you can. Put your fruit into your mouth, but don't chew it yet, just savor it. Feel the earth. Feel the solidity. Feel the resilience. Dig your fingers into the earth. Hold the dirt in your hand. Give thanks for the bounty of the land. Give thanks for the land itself—for the countless plants and animals that have created our rich soil over the eons. Tighten your mouth around the fruit and let its juices run down your throat. Give thanks for the taste and the nourishment. Give thanks for all of life.

Gratitude that I'm Me

I am a unique expression of the universal fabric of creation, I am that I am that I am.

In the eternity of all creation, I am the only me that ever will be, and I am so honored that the power of the Universe has chosen for me to be me.

The world is a better place because I am here. The energy that I radiate into this world is a gift beyond my own understanding.

Through me, an all-encompassing love enters this world, and I am profoundly grateful that the Powers of Light have chosen me to be a conduit for infinite love.

I am simultaneously me—an independent being of free will and bold courage, and me—an integral and inseparable element of the web of timeless creation.

I am a paradox—a duality—and yet an entirely unified me.

I am a miracle, and that's why I'm me.

Gratitude for the Human Spirit

The human spirit ranges across a truly amazing diversity of experiences and emotions—the highest peaks and the lowest valleys.

One minute we merge in awe with the compassionate creative universal force, and the next minute our biology focuses us toward other aspects of our human existence.

Each of us is loving in some moments—hateful in others. Patient and calm sometimes—harried by urgency at others. Understanding—and self-absorbed. Reassuring—and sarcastic. Generous—and greedy. Trusting—and jealous. Comforting—and snappish. Original—and stuck in a rut. Thankful—and needy. Forgiving—and vengeful. Nurturing ourselves—and stuffing ourselves with fast food. Honoring our bodies—and over-stressing. Being joyful—and suffering.

What does all this mean? It means only that we are human—nothing more. Our opportunity is to love ourselves exactly as we are—with all our joys and sufferings. To be grateful for everything. To forgive ourselves for doubting our own worthiness—for we have no need to be anything other than what we are.

THANKSGIVING AS A SOURCE OF JOY

Thanksgiving Day is my favorite holiday, the one with the deepest meaning to me. Gratitude is one of our deepest bonds with the Infinite. Setting aside a day to celebrate our gratitude for food, family, friends, and all our other blessings is a magnificent tradition.

Every day, we have so much for which to be grateful. Let each day be a Thanksgiving—a day to acknowledge our food, our family, our friends, our homes, our health, our very lives.

Food is a perfect symbol for all our gratitudes. It's tangible, it can be very enjoyable, and it is something we require every day. Whereas losing the companionship of friends and family would be a dull ache that grew over time, the absence of food becomes a sharp pain in a day or two, and would become fatal within a few weeks—as was an annual reality at the time of the Plymouth Thanksgiving.

Raise a bowl of food in Thanksgiving. Let your thanks for the food symbolize your thanks for all of life. Let your whole being merge with the Universe in gratitude.

ABUNDANCE—GRATITUDE FOR MIRACULOUS GIFTS

When we perceive an abundance of something, we relax in the assurance that we will never lack for that thing. Abundance is not proportional to the amount of something we have. I can enjoy financial abundance on my social security check, or I can live in fear of lack with millions of dollars in the bank.

Abundance and gratitude work in a positive, reinforcing cycle. When I sense the abundance with which I have been blessed, I am profoundly grateful—when I am grateful for what I have, I experience increasing abundance.

Love and unity with Spirit and all creation is the most miraculous gift of all. Limitless. Always available in abundant profusion. It is ironic that we so often sense a lack of love. Some of us live lives of desperation, believing that we are unloved and unlovable, and will always be so. Know that love is always abundant—when we are willing to open our hearts and receive that love with gratitude.

> I close my eyes and let my feeling of unity with all creation
> envelope me. I am grateful for the world. I am grateful for
> Spirit. I am grateful for my life—my very existence. I am
> grateful for this day—for this moment.

A List of Gratitudes

I find great power in listing my gratitudes. Every time I repeat this exercise, I find renewed inspiration and connection with the Infinite. My list begins:

> I am grateful to be alive and *me* in this instant. I'm grateful
> for everything that has ever occurred to bring me to this
> moment of being exactly who I am today. I'm grateful to my
> distant ancestors who survived eons of sameness punctuated
> by moments of terror . . . who fought fearsome beasts and

barely survived each winter in order to pass down the genes that make me who I am today.

I am grateful to my father's father who sailed from China alone as a young boy in the hold of a sailing ship, bringing my genes from desperate hunger to the opportunity of America. I am grateful to my father's mother and her ancestors who brought their part of my biological inheritance from Holland to New Amsterdam. I am grateful to my mother's parents who brought their share of my genes from an unhappy Germany to a new beginning in Connecticut.

I am grateful to my parents for choosing to bring me into the world—seventeen years after my only sibling, and at an age when most couples of their generation had completed their childbearing. Just genetically, my chances of being me are infinitesimally small.

I am grateful for everything my parents did and didn't do. I am grateful for the unconditional love I received from each of them. I am grateful for the lessons of my father's heavy drinking, and my mother's fear of strangers. I am grateful both for the joy of my mother's generous readings and other attentions to me, and for the pain my isolated early childhood later caused me.

I am grateful even for the bullying and other painful experiences of my youth, as each one made me the person I am today. I am grateful for every success and every failure I have ever had . . . every new love and every ending . . . every promotion and every firing . . . every smile and every tear.

TODAY IN MY WORLD:

Consider recording, daily, everything you like best about yourself and the qualities for which you are especially grateful. After doing that for several days: write a gratitude piece about yourself. Or just make a short list of what you are most grateful for today.

Pay It Forward

While many of us recognize the expression, "Pay it forward," from Catherine Ryan Hyde's book and the 2000 movie of that name, the concept is an old one. Benjamin Franklin described the process:

> I do not pretend to give such a Sum; I only lend it to you.... When you meet with another honest Man in similar Distress, you must pay me by lending this Sum to him; enjoining him to discharge the Debt by a like operation, when he shall be able, and shall meet with another opportunity. I hope it may thus go thro' many hands, before it meets with a Knave that will stop its Progress. This is a trick of mine for doing a deal of good with a little money.

The words "pay it forward" are used by Robert A. Heinlein in his 1951 book *Between Planets* to describe this concept—perhaps the first use of this phrase.

We have reason to have infinite gratitude to the Universe for everything we have and everything we are, yet we cannot repay the Universe. We have gratitude for our distant ancestors, yet cannot repay them. We have gratitude to our parents for our life, and to our parents or other caregivers for our nurture, yet we cannot repay them in kind. We have many other gratitudes that, for one reason or another, cannot be repaid to those who were so generous to us.

To express that gratitude, pay it forward. The nature of life is that we pay forward our biological creation and nurture. Our parents gift us with life and nurture, and we gift our children with life and nurture. While this much is essential to continued human existence, choose to take pay it forward further—much further.

Consider making pay it forward a way of life. As we have observed many times, expectation is always a cause of suffering.

Rather than expecting to be repaid when we loan something to someone, consider the loans we make to be forward payments for the loans we received from our ancestors, nurturers, and others. Request that any loan that we make be repaid forward, when the recipient is able, and then completely forget about the loan. It is no longer our business if, when, or how the loan is repaid— or is not repaid.

MAR   Have gratitude in all things. Not a suck-it-up-and-pretend-it's-a-good-thing gratitude, but the kind of gratitude that contributes to a circular sense of life: that all things have contributed to who you are in this moment. And if you like who you are, then it follows you will have a sense of gratitude for the whole of the experiences that brought you to this place.

Chapter 6

CHOICE—With Open Mind and Heart

AFFIRMATION I Choose with Open Mind and Open Heart—I renounce all assumptions and expectations, and I declare that I will thoughtfully consider all possibilities. I will choose with courage, awareness, consciousness, and compassion toward all. ॐ

One man's theology is another man's belly laugh.
—Robert A. Heinlein

I release myself from the choices and history of others. I do not condemn myself to the sorrows of another, nor do I bind myself by anyone else's expectations.

—mar

There is nothing I ever need to have.
There is nothing I ever need to do.
I say no to the demands of the world.
I say yes to the longings of my own heart.
—jlh

JLH Do you believe that everything you did today was a conscious free-will choice? If so, here's a wake-up call. Most of the time, we do what we do and think what we think because that's what we did yesterday, because that's what our parents did, or because that's what is done or thought in our community.

Often, we are not fully conscious and are not truly exercising our free will. We live our lives out of habit, addicted to our entrenched ways of living, virtually unconscious to what happens around us. It doesn't have to be that way.

We have the ability to break free of our past and of the social influences that surround us. We can choose personal freedom—we can choose to live joyfully.

JOY IS A CHOICE

W.I.C? Who's In Charge:
. . . of your day?
. . . of your feelings?
. . . of your goals?
. . . of your activities?
. . . of your state of being?
In the midst of the flurry—clarity.
In the midst of the storm—calm.
In the midst of divided interests—certainty.
In the many roads—a clear choice.

—mar

Everything we do is a choice. In every instant, we are making a choice about what we will do in that instant (as well as a choice about what we will think in that instant). We may choose to turn off and shut down our conscious attention, allowing the autopilot of our habits and instincts to make our choices, but they are still choices.

Why not make all your choices with consciousness—from the longings of your own heart? Wipe the cobwebs of boredom and inattention from your eyes. Forget everything you think you know. Open your eyes wide and look—really look—deeply at all of life. See the world with new eyes.

Say *no* to the demands of the world. Stop to ask why this demand *needs* to be fulfilled. What is the need, and on whose authority has the need been established?

Take responsibility for the consequences of your choices. Choose with conscious awareness, and your choices will lead to joy.

MY MIND: BRILLIANT FRIEND AND INSIDIOUS FOE

Perhaps you have never considered that there is a you that is separate from your mind. Or perhaps you recognize that your mind is only one aspect of yourself, but you believe that you are in charge of your mind.

If you believe you are always in charge of your mind—or that you *are* your mind, try this experiment:

TODAY IN MY WORLD:

Get up a half hour earlier than usual tomorrow, and go for a walk around the neighborhood—alone, and in complete silence—leaving the iPod and cell phone at home.

For the first half of the walk, just observe your surroundings, and observe your thoughts and stories about the things you see on your walk.

On the second half of the walk, try to keep your mind blank—no thinking, no stories, no explanations for anything.

When you let your thoughts roll, what stories did you create? What irritated you, and what stories did you create about why it irritated you? Were you able to stop the stories when you tried? It is unlikely that you could stop your stories for a full fifteen minutes.

The nature of being human is to create nonstop stories. For everything we observe or experience, we create a story—not sometimes, but always.

That chatter in our heads that just won't stop is called monkey mind. *Monkey mind* is a Buddhist term describing mental activity that is unsettled, restless, capricious, unpredictable, confused, uncontrollable. Our monkey mind constantly invents stories to explain everything we see and hear. Each human being is the owner of an unstoppable monkey mind.

Monkey mind, monkey mind, chatter away.
You stay with me always, you clutter my day.
There's no silence around when you talk in my head,
and you never shut up, and you won't till I'm dead.
—jlh

We can interrupt our monkey mind for a brief time, but soon it gets triggered again and restarts its story making. While we can never stop our monkey mind, we can learn to tame it. The first step is simply recognizing its existence. Once we acknowledge our monkey mind, we can just say thank you whenever it chatters, consciously think a positive thought, and continue boldly through our day.

An irony of the term *monkey mind* is that the mind chatter so named is a uniquely human experience. Monkeys at play are in constant physical motion—twisting, wriggling, intertwining—but as far as we know, the minds of those playful monkeys remain focused on the present moment—without regret, guilt, or shame over the past, and without anxiety over any possible future.

Question Your Questions

Are you ever stuck on a question for which you can't find an acceptable answer? That is a good time to consider asking a different question. Every question is based on some assumptions—usually assumptions that we don't see unless we go looking. Questioning the question often shines a light on the assumptions underlying the question and allows us to break through our stuck-ness.

How can I get my boss to give me the raise I deserve and need? is the sort of question that appears to have no answer. Question the question. What are my priorities in life? How do I value money relative to play, family, friends, health? How could I redesign my life to need less money? Whatever your questions are, question them.

MAR People ask how to know what questions to ask when beginning to question assumptions. In *Philosophy in a New Key,* Susanne Langer said, "If we would have new knowledge, we must get a whole world of new questions."

I interviewed a dozen candidates for the position of manager of my new retail store. I hired my final interviewee, Meg, on the spot. Smart. Savvy. She had qualities that held her above all the others. A fearless curiosity and unrestrained willingness. Meg loved to learn. Her enthusiasm seemed boundless. She had little fear, and she was willing to try/learn/explore anything that she judged had merit.

I asked her to do a broad spectrum of tasks requiring many different skill sets. When Meg didn't know how to do what I asked her to do, she considered educating herself on the specifics just part of the process of what she needed to know to do the job.

Meg's style led me to ask her about it. How very simple her answer was: "When I'm not sure how to do something, I am certain to have a whole bunch of questions. The questions lead me, teach me where I need to look to find out what I need to know."

Rainer Maria Rilke wrote in *Letters to a Young Poet* that you should:

> Have patience with everything unresolved in your heart and try to love the questions themselves. . . . Don't search for the answers, which could not be given to you now, because you would not be able to live them. And the point is to live everything. Live the questions now. Perhaps then, someday far in the future, you will gradually, without even noticing it, live your way into the answer.

In any regard that you would like to discover new knowledge, create a whole new world of questions for you to live into—and, when you're ready, you'll live into answers. It is easy to allow questions to confuse your process—if you believe that all questions must have answers. In the process of choice and perception, asking questions for their own sake becomes a clarifying tool.

Mind Fog

JLH Fog is many things. It can be the soft, comfortable gray blanket that sneaks up to insulate us from reality and to supply a reason for choosing to remain indoors and enjoy hot chocolate, a bathrobe, and slippers in place of mowing the grass or going for a jog. The fog of atmospheric inversion is a time of danger as well. Freeways are a notoriously unfortunate place to experience fog. Ships don't do well with fog either. Fog is also a condition of the mind that, most of the time, most of us would prefer to avoid. Alzheimer's or a stroke—no thanks. A couple of drinks—perhaps.

Mind fog affects us all from time to time. We're sleepy, we're partying, a virus tackled us, we're just relaxed and happy—great, no reason to be sharp at every instant. Never being sharp, however, makes for a pretty dull life.

Some of us have unconsciously gotten into the habit of continuous mind fog—a lazy habit that insidiously overtakes our consciousness. Why think about making choices today when I can just do what I did yesterday? Why listen to that other political candidate—I've always been a _____ (fill in the blank) and moreover, all my friends are. Why pay attention to the sights and sounds as I walk to work? I've walked this same route every day for the last five years. Hmmm . . . might we be missing something?

MAR Every one of the eight points of Simply an Inspired Life has to do with being awake. Living an observed life. Noticing.

We Don't See What We're Not Looking For

JLH I had the pleasure of attending a talk by Dr. Michael Shermer, author of *How We Believe,* during which he showed a video of a basketball game. Before the video, he instructed the audience to count the number of times the white team passed the ball. After the video, Shermer asked the audience how many times the ball had been passed and then asked how many people in the audience had seen the gorilla walking across the basketball court. Not even half the hands went up. When the video was replayed, the man in the gorilla suit was obvious. We are all conditioned to see only what we are looking for—especially if we are looking very attentively, as when counting basketball passes.

Alexander Green, author of the wonderful free e-mail newsletter *Spiritual Wealth*, tells another story about not seeing what is right in front of us. Green writes of a world-renowned violin player performing on a New York street corner, while a thousand New Yorkers—who would have paid hundreds of dollars to see him perform at Carnegie Hall—walked past without pausing to listen.

Why do we not see what is right in front of us and which is perfectly obvious when pointed out?

We always see what we are looking for—we seldom see what we are not looking for. Even more disconcerting, we often see what we are looking for, even if it is not there. If we are looking for trouble, we will see trouble anywhere and everywhere.

Sharpening Our Perception

The dictionary has several definitions of the word *perception*, but the one we're going to focus on is "the ability to notice or discern things that escape the notice of most people." Most of us really don't pay much attention to what is going on around us, most of the time. Sometimes, as in the gorilla story above, it is because we are so focused on a detail that we miss the big picture. Most of the time, though, it is because we are what might euphemistically be called "lost in thought." It's not really thought, though, but we certainly are lost.

What passes for thought is usually a stream of snippets about past and future time—regrets, worries, fears, and resentments, with a sprinkling of hopes, wishes, and dreams thrown in—all courtesy of our monkey mind.

Sharpening our perception requires that we develop the ability to refocus our attention back to the present. Like most skills, this one requires concentration and practice. Whenever the stream of snippets starts whirring past like a movie, recognize it, thank it, and refocus back onto the present.

Sharpening our perception gives us an opening to become aware of what the people in our lives are actually doing and saying. When we are lost in thought, our experience of listening to a conversation goes something like this (with the stream of snippets in *italics*): "On my way over here, the idiot driver in front of me slammed on his brakes, and ..." *I hate people who don't know how to drive. Sunday drivers are the worst. Always driving too slow ...* "I wasn't too badly hurt, however, just a bruise on ..." *My foot still hurts from where I kicked the lawnmower last week. The stupid thing wouldn't start, and my toe is still black and blue, and I really need to have the blade sharpened, and ...*

Go ahead and laugh—this is life. When was the last time you checked out of a conversation and gave control to your monkey mind? Probably not that long ago. It is human nature to run our own stream of snippets most of the time. And when we do, we can't even hear what anyone else is saying, let alone empathize with their emotions and humanity.

Threshold of Perception

We are either aware of something or we aren't—there is no in between. If we are not aware of the man in the gorilla suit, he is below our threshold of perception and, for us, simply does not exist. Once he passes our threshold of perception, not only does he exist, but we can't get rid of him. We can never again see that scene without seeing the gorilla man. First we couldn't see him because we weren't looking for him—then we can't stop seeing him once we know he is there.

Understanding the threshold of perception may allow us to be kinder when our spouse looks up after we have been speaking for thirty seconds and asks, "Did you say something?" It can also serve as a reminder that we tune out and become deaf to the world rather frequently.

Evolution Has Not Always Been Kind to the Human Spirit

As far as we know, animals are completely focused on the present moment, and they act instinctively. Sometimes these instincts are remarkably powerful and specific. Salmon return to the river of their birth, and some birds follow precise migration patterns for thousands of miles.

Life is not so simple for us humans. Somewhere along the evolutionary line, we lost many of our beneficial instinctive behaviors. In ceasing to follow our instincts, we stopped taking actions that would maximize our well-being and happiness, and we became addicted to measuring our every action, and even thought, against an ill-defined set of cultural values. From family to tribe to chiefdom to nation, we have subjected ourselves to an increasingly arbitrary set of rules and increasingly complex social structures to enforce those rules.

The overlapping rule systems of our society are vague and constantly changing. It is no wonder most of us constantly feel we have failed at something and are stricken by guilt and shame. This spider web of rules includes the tens of thousands of pages of laws enacted by governments at various levels, the requirements and injunctions inflicted by organized religion and other social institutions, and the explicit and implicit demands and prohibitions of our traditions, community, and family.

Do I advocate breaking the law? No way! Mostly, I do not even advocate going against the traditions and expectations of our community and family. The issue lies in *why* we follow, or don't follow, the explicit and implicit rules of our community. Is it from blind habit or from considered choice?

The only logical reason for any action is to optimize the results. Going to prison or paying a fine is virtually never an optimum result. Living in a community or family that is seriously upset with us is seldom an optimum result either.

The crucial issue here is making logical choices that optimize our results. Following the laws and expectations of the society in which we live is usually a logical way to maximize our happiness and minimize our pain. Be very clear, however, that there is no inherent rightness or wrongness involved in the vast majority of legal statutes, and even less absolute truth in the strictures of church and family.

Other than murder and assault, I am hard-pressed to think of any prohibitions I would consider as even approaching absolute truth. Theft, you say? I am in a remote town. My child will die within a few hours without a medicine that is stocked by the town's only drugstore. The pharmacy is closed, and the druggist refuses to reopen. I break in and steal the medicine. Did I break a natural and universal law? I could argue either side of this specific example, but my overarching conclusion is that there simply is no *absolute* right or wrong in nature. Right and wrong are human concepts that are unique to a specific society and time in history.

OPENING TO NEW PERSPECTIVES

Over the years, we have come to see life as we expect it to be. We have made assumptions about how things are—and that has saved us a lot of thinking. We've made expectations of others and of ourselves based on those assumptions. We've thought we knew the rules of life, and that also saved us a lot of thinking.

What if today was the day to shed the scales from your eyes? What if today was the day to renounce all assumptions and expectations, and declare: "I will thoughtfully consider all possibilities and *choose* among them with consciousness."

What if today was the day to bring a childlike wonder and a beginner mind to life?

Beginner mind is a Zen Buddhist term for an open-mindedness that enables us to move past our assumptions of the nature of life to really see our surroundings and our community with new eyes.

Everyone believes that their beliefs are the right ones— that is why they are called beliefs.

—jlh

It is instructive to examine our most deeply held beliefs. These are the kind of beliefs that we don't even call beliefs—because, for us, they are just the way things *are.*

For many people, the absolute truth of the so-called Golden Rule is one of those deeply held beliefs that are beyond any possible question.

I invite you to suspend your judgments for five minutes and adopt a beginner mind as you read the following section. My intention is to incite you to think—really think—about your values. Whatever you conclude after reading this is OK—more than OK—just focus on being open and thinking consciously, rather than just reacting with: "But my parents, priest, teachers, family, friends, neighbors, government officials say . . ."

The Golden Rule is *Not* Golden

The so-called Golden Rule occurs in many forms and in multiple cultures. The version in Matthew 7:12, "So in everything, do to others what you would have them do to you," is reasonably representative. The Golden Rule has been praised as the basis of morality and saintliness, so how could any responsible person even suggest that it is not "golden?"

Start with some examples: Things I would like others to do for me include feeding me if I'm hungry, treating my ailments if I'm sick, and providing a warm and dry place for me to sleep if I'm cold and wet. These are probably all things others would want me to do for them. I would also like others to serve me a rare steak, hold the onions on my salad, and use real butter on my baked potato. Taken literally, the Golden Rule dictates that I should serve my vegetarian friend a rare steak, and my dieting friend lots of butter.

Given the trivial nature of this first example, you may be tempted to respond: "You're being too literal. The Golden Rule really asks that we treat others as *they* want to be treated." Hmmm . . . if that's what the Golden Rule means, why doesn't it just say so? But it doesn't—in any of its occurrences.

Next example: For me, treating my ailments if I'm sick would definitely include providing me with blood transfusions if I were severely anemic or had lost a lot of blood in a car accident. If I applied the Golden Rule to my neighbor's similar condition, I would donate my own blood and rush him to the hospital for a transfusion. Suppose, however, that my neighbor has a deeply held religious injunction against blood transfusions. Hmmm . . .

The killer (literally) example comes when my neighbor's one-year-old daughter gets severe anemia. Ooops . . . no way out. You probably have a very good answer for this dilemma, but I guarantee that whatever your answer is, it will reflect your own history and personal beliefs. You may believe that the Golden Rule charges you to allow your neighbor his religious freedom—as you would want him to allow you your freedom. Or, you may believe that the Golden Rule charges you to attempt to provide the one-year-old with the "superior" medical care that you would want others to provide to you. In either case, there is no absolute, natural, or God-given moral answer to this dilemma.

However well-intentioned, the Golden Rule is often more harmful than helpful and has led to much personal misery as well as to some of the world's greatest tragedies. If I believe that my religion is the only one that can get you to Heaven, then the Golden Rule says I must convert you, whatever it takes—right? Remember the Crusades and the Salem Witch Trials as two examples among many.

Almost any sect, cult, or religion will legislate its creed into law if it acquires the political power to do so.
—Robert A. Heinlein

Like me, you probably first react to the Heinlein quote by focusing on the word *almost* and thinking that those other people would corrupt the political process with their parochial beliefs, but *I* would never do that.

Hogwash! The Heinlein quote should have the *almost* removed entirely!

Further, I believe that I would never advocate laws that favor one spiritual belief system over another—after all, I'm a strong supporter of the First Amendment ("Congress shall make no law respecting an establishment of religion, or prohibiting the free exercise thereof").

Double hogwash!

As you may have observed from my comments above, my personal belief system requires that I advocate laws that children are "entitled to modern medical care—with or without the consent of their parents." To me that doesn't *feel* like "legislate its creed into law." It feels, to me, like being loving, human, and humane—and who could object? Well...as you saw above, absolutely everyone with a different spiritual creed from mine would object vigorously.

But I'm right, and they're wrong.

Really?

That's the whole point. We all believe that *our* beliefs are the right ones—that is why they are called beliefs.

TODAY IN MY WORLD:

Take a few minutes to write your feelings and thoughts about this challenge against the Golden Rule. Are you angry? Upset? How do you feel about the preceding section? How do you feel about the Golden Rule now?

If the Golden Rule isn't a reasonable bedrock for morality, what is? I offer two possibilities for you to consider: the cynical view that there simply is no morality, and the humanitarian view that compassion is the bedrock of morality. By choosing the humanitarian view, we can have compassion both for the anemic toddler *and* for her parent.

REVITALIZE YOUR THINKING

MAR There's an aphorism that has grown out of the twelve-step movement, and it is widely delivered when someone keeps making the same mistake. The phrase is, "It's your best thinking that got you here." If we don't like where we are, then we need to redirect our thinking to help us get elsewhere; our best thinking up till now is no longer effective. The pivot point to opening to new perspectives is knowing how to access those perspectives. To shift or revitalize your best thinking so it can take you to a different place. It takes a lot of effort. You are, essentially, retraining a muscle.

Here are the technicalities of a process I teach. It is called the Radmacher Innovator Process, but it could also be titled Opening to New Perspectives. With this methodology you will create a tool, utterly unique to you, that will assist you as you work to open to a new way of seeing and thinking.

You will need a stack of small pieces of paper in three different colors. I prefer to use lined 3 x 5-inch index cards which I have my local print shop cut in half. This leaves me with a nice stack of 3 x 2½-inch cards. You will identify a list in each of three categories:

1. Role/function of a board of directors of either a nonprofit, a corporation, or both. If you are unfamiliar with a board's process, do some research and ask associates who serve on boards what their responsibilities involve.

2. Your personal heroes and role models, living or dead, real or imagined, animate or inanimate.

3. Your greatest strengths and the strengths and qualities that you wish to develop but that aren't at full strength yet.

Assign each category a color. Each item will be written on one of the small color-coded cards.

I'll use an example from the board of directors function category.

Choose the color of cards for this category and start writing out all the roles, responsibilities, and functions you can think of that a board performs. Write only one function per card. If the board's job is to hire and fire, that would be two cards—hire top-level management, and fire top-level management. Others might be: establish job descriptions, create facility plan, write budget. In addition to specific functions, you can also list the various titles of board members on these cards (i.e. president, treasurer, etc.).

Assign another color to the second category, personal heroes and role models. Here as well, write out only one role per card.

As you complete the qualities and strengths categories fill them out generously, but don't strain. Attempt to have close to an equal number in each category. For example, five board roles, fifty heroes and ten qualities would not be desirable. But thirty, twenty-eight, and and thirty-nine would be a good balance.

Write out your cards with permanent ink. You don't want your words to run if you spill something on them. Writing these cards out makes the process more personal. Using typeface makes them more readable. Use whatever mechanism is most accessible to you. When you have three nice stacks of color-coded cards written on, you are ready to use this to open your thinking to new perspectives.

Have you ever seen one of those electronic slot penny machines? They have three drums spinning in different directions, and when they come to a stop there are three images facing forward. That's just how this innovation process works. Each color stack can be considered one of those rotating drums.

Think of a project that's stumped you, a friendship that's befuddled you, an organizational issue that's caused you tremendous angst. Call to mind any issue at all for which you lack immediate clarity. Focus on one particular issue, and draw a card from each color pile.

The three cards, in partnership, form a matrix of process innovation. Address your issue from this point of view. For example, from my process innovator I have drawn three cards, one from each color: Acting as **president**, (the board title) **Eleanor Roosevelt** (a heroine of mine) is going to use extraordinary **prioritizing skills** (quality category) to resolve my concern as to how to balance my time between now and when I leave on my next book tour.

I choose to use a letter format in this exercise. Knowing Eleanor Roosevelt, as I do, through reading her journals, records of her letters, and numerous biographies, I know she would encourage me in this way:

> My Dearest Friend, Mary Anne:
>
> There are many burdens all of us bear. They each have different sounds, but what they have in common is that we alone are responsible to see that they are dispatched with efficiency and ease. I would encourage you to dispense the most difficult thing first. Be strong and do the thing you think you cannot do. After that task is completed, everything else will seem so much easier. And in dealing with your many responsibilities in this manner, you will discover the least important ones do manage to drop to the bottom of your task list, rather than getting the most attention. I do encourage you to fortify yourself and to be clear on the tasks that will be most in line with your true mission in life. Remember, you can call on your friends at any time. In your hour of need, we will always help you in whatever way we can. If you find yourself close to departure time and have too much on your plate, ask for help. I know I will assist in any way I can, and I think I speak for all of us.
>
> With great affection,
> Eleanor

By opening myself to a fresh view through this Innovator Process, I have several helpful epiphanies: doing the difficult things first makes all the other tasks seem easier; I can measure my priorities in the light of my larger life mission; if I run out of time before I run out of tasks, at least I left the least important things to last; if I am stumped, I can ask my friends for help.

I chose to use a letter format this time. I could have used other processes to innovate perspective. A memo, recipe, invitation, announcement, brochure, structure-tree, movie synopsis, dialogue, loudspeaker announcement, emergency broadcast. The Process Innovator is easily applied to family and professional applications, and I've used it in my teaching work. It has benefitted, over the years, by clients providing input and giving additional examples of how it can be used. I share it joyfully with you and encourage you to broaden its impact by making full use of it and sharing it with others.

Prejudice

Prejudice—an opinion formed beforehand based on incomplete knowledge, emotional feelings, and/or stereotypes.

JLH The word *prejudice* has become virtually an obscenity—it is considered a strong accusation to call someone prejudiced. Can there be anything about prejudice that isn't bad? Actually, yes.

The human race couldn't have survived without prejudices. If a lion mauls my father, I am likely to develop a strong prejudice against all lions. Prejudices like that have saved humanity's collective scrawny ass many times. Maybe the next lion I met would lay down with the lambs, but my own prejudice would cause me to run like heck back to my tree or cave or whatever.

Prejudice is a two-edged sword. Like the steel sort of sword, it is very sharp, very useful, and very dangerous if not properly mastered. Everything we say, do, think, and feel is a product of our personal history and the collective history of humankind. Our name for these histories is *prejudice.*

We start getting prejudices the moment we are born—it is a consequence of acquiring a history. The best we can ever hope for is to recognize and accept our own prejudices. Once we accept that we all have prejudices, and always will, we can factor their presence into our awareness and our conscious choices.

Consider Choosing Your Value System

Mostly, people don't choose their value systems. Our parents had a value system. Our community has, in most cases, if not a single value system, at least a very narrow range of value systems. Rather than consciously choosing our values, most of us have just assumed the value systems that surround us.

I am not advocating that you make any changes in your value system or lifestyle—I am neither for it nor against it. What I am advocating is conscious choice. Wake up. Don't be a mindless follower. Think for yourself. Choose for yourself. Whatever your choice, let it be *your* own choice.

Value Systems Evolve

While it may take generations or centuries, value systems do evolve. Our American value system no longer supports burning accused witches as it did only four hundred years ago, dueling as it did two hundred years ago, or segregation as it did fifty years ago.

When John Lennon chose to study with a guru in India in the 1960s, the general societal reaction was outrage. Parents who had barely tolerated the Beatles' innovative music and hair styles, now forbade their children to buy Beatles albums based on the sacrilegious depravity of studying with an Eastern holy man. Forty years later, a celebrity following a guru isn't even newsworthy, and perhaps half of Americans would no longer consider it depraved if a son or daughter left for a year's pilgrimage to India.

Majority rule only works if you're also considering individual rights, because you can't have five wolves and one sheep voting on what to have for supper.
—Larry Flynt

Today, roughly half of Americans do not accept the overwhelming evidence for evolution, roughly half favor constitutional amendments discriminating against citizens based on sexual preference, and roughly half of Americans believe terminally ill patients should be kept alive against their will. What does the future hold? The outcome is clear. Progress always wins. The question is how quickly humans will evolve. Have patience! Have compassion! Have compassion for everyone, regardless of their beliefs!

Consider Choosing Science *and* Spirit

While some people consider science and spirituality to be adversaries, there is actually no overlap between the domains they profess to explain.

Science does not even attempt to explain the cause of anything. Science merely quantifies and documents the relationships among miracles. For example, the Law of Gravitation relates the mass of two objects, and the distance between them, to the force with which they attract each other. That is simply a relationship among miracles. It doesn't say *why* mass, distance, and gravitational force are related in the way they are, or even why gravity exists at all, or why mass exists, or distance exists, or energy, or time, or anything else.

The word *why* is often associated with science, as in the question, "Why is the sky blue?" The answer that science would give—something about blue light being absorbed and then re-radiated by molecules in the air—is not a *why* answer; it is a *how* answer.

The definition of *why* is "for what reason or purpose." Look again at the scientific explanation for the sky appearing blue. It has nothing to do with giving a reason or purpose. I am trained in science and engineering, and I continue to be fascinated by all the relationships science has discovered. I remain curious about finding new relationships, and I cheer whenever more is learned about black holes or another Lucy skeleton is discovered and analyzed. I am also very clear about the limitations of science. Science is great with relationships and logic, but never has and never will address the meaning of anything—the reason for being.

When we really want an answer that addresses meaning, we have entered the realm of spirituality. Every belief about why we and the Universe exist as we do is a spiritual belief—atheism is a spiritual belief in that it offers an answer for the meaning of our existence. Spirituality comes in an almost infinite variety of flavors and is a profoundly personal choice. We often hold highly conflicting beliefs, and we will always differ about beliefs because, by definition, beliefs cannot be proven. Just be clear that when you disagree with someone's *why* answer, you are simply stating that the two of you hold differing spiritual beliefs. Choose to recognize the difference and leave science out of your argument.

MAR In all things and in all ways, choice impacts virtually every element of our life. It bears repeating that even those things which seem out of reach of our choice are governed by how we choose to perceive them.

Chapter 7
VISION—With Powerful Intention

AFFIRMATION I Dream with Powerful Intention—Opening my mind to Spirit, I trust my intuition to deliver powerful visions of my inspired future, and I empower my intent to transform those visions into reality. ॐ

Our deepest fear is not that we are inadequate. Our deepest fear is that we are powerful beyond measure.
—Marianne Williamson

Vision stands on the shoulders of what is actual to get a better view of what is possible.
—mar

I am the call.
From far beyond this life,
I hear the call.
From place beyond all place,
I feel the call.
From time before all time,
I know the call.
From one before all ones,
I am the call.
—jlh

JLH We are called. We are all called from beyond all place and time, by a power beyond all power. When you close your eyes, relax your shoulders, and spread your arms wide, you can feel the call. The call says, "You are here for a reason. Your life is important."

The caller remains anonymous. We refrain from asking for a name. God? Our ancestors? Gaia? Spirit? Random biochemistry? Questions aside, focus on the message: There is a purpose to your life. Find your purpose.

Life is without meaning. You bring the meaning to it.
The meaning of life is whatever you ascribe it to be.
—Joseph Campbell

Paradox is at work here. We have a palpable sense that there is purpose to our lives, and yet, objectively, our lives serve no purpose. Not only our own lives, but the entire existence of humanity is without inherent meaning. We, everyone who we will ever know, and all of humanity will one day be reduced to cosmic dust—nothing more.

So why not just throw up our hands in despair and surrender to the utter meaninglessness of our lives?

The point of the Joseph Campbell quote is *not* that our lives are meaningless or purposeless, but rather that it is our job to find the meaning in our own life—to *choose* the purpose of our life.

Perhaps you are inclined to reply that all lives have the same purpose and that some particular book outlines that purpose.

At least for the time that you are reading this chapter, put aside everything that you believe about the purpose of human life, and take this opportunity to deeply examine your choice for the purpose of your life—the only life you can make choices about, the only life you truly have any influence over, the life that creates your experience of joy or of suffering.

TO FIND YOUR PURPOSE, CHOOSE YOUR PURPOSE

If you are willing to consider the question of choosing a unique personal purpose for your life, begin by asking yourself these questions:

What are my dreams?
What are my dreams for the world?
What are my dreams for my personal future?

These are some of the biggest questions you will ever get to ask yourself.

Our dreams are only limited by our lack of willingness to fly our thoughts from possibility to reality.

—mar

TODAY IN MY WORLD:
Take a deep breath, close your eyes, and visualize the world in 2200—long after you and everyone you know has passed on. What do you see? Do you see people loving each other and in a state of conscious joy? Or suffering—perhaps people destroying each other? Have we humans blown ourselves to smithereens? Are we well fed and using abundant clean-energy sources? Or

are we starving and stranded from having run out of food and oil? Have we controlled overpopulation, or does Earth resemble a rabbit warren?

Returning to the present, how do you desire your life to move the future of the world toward joy and away from suffering? What is your personal dream for the future of the entire human race?

What is the importance of having a vision for the distant future—a future that will transpire long after you have died? Without a clear idea of how you want the world to evolve, you can't very well move down a path toward achieving it.

Your vision for the future is significant in three ways:

1. Your vision inspires the actions you take in life.
2. Your vision holds a powerful energy of intent. There is a force that listens to your intent and calls it into being. Never underestimate the power of that force to turn your intent into reality. Your compassionate intent benefits all humanity as well as yourself, while your harmful intent is mirrored back to you as intense suffering—mostly, but not completely, sparing others.
3. There is a huge multiplier effect on group intent. Ten people with the same compassionate intent are powerful. A thousand are almost unstoppable. The force of your energetic intention merges with the energies of all those with similar intent. At some threshold—at some critical mass—that intention gains a life of its own. It's as if a few thousand raindrops could join forces to create the mighty Mississippi. Imagine if a billion people focused their intent on a joyful and loving future . . .

Your intention for the future of the world does matter.

My Dream for My Own Future

Did you begin this book with a clear vision for your own future? Or did you have no idea even of your plans for next week? Either way, right now is a good time to put aside both your plans and your uncertainties regarding your future, and undertake the exercise of dreaming a future for yourself. You may or may not ever succeed in creating the future you dream, but if you don't have a dream, you most certainly will never create a future that you find inspiring. Moreover, if you don't have a dream, you will miss the challenge and joy of the journey in following your dream.

Powerful dreams inspire powerful action.
—jlh

TODAY IN MY WORLD:

Set aside an hour and find a quiet, comfortable place. Outdoors under a tree on a warm Sunday afternoon would be ideal, but any quiet place will be more than good enough.

If you have one, use a voice recorder to record your thoughts as you dream your future. In addition, have pen and paper by your side to record the highlights.

Lie back, close your eyes, and breathe deeply and slowly. It is good to be warm, relaxed, comfortable, and a little sleepy, but if you fall fast asleep, just have a good nap today and start dreaming your future again tomorrow.

Let the visions come . . . Full-color motion pictures with sound . . . Where are you? What are you doing? Who is with you? What are the smells? The tastes? How do you feel? What are you wearing? What is going on around you? What is making you happy? What is making you feel fulfilled?

Let your voice recorder run—vocalize everything that streams through your mind. Talk to yourself and don't stop. If you don't have a voice recorder, talk out loud to yourself anyway. If you have a thought you really don't want to chance forgetting, write it down, but mostly just keep dreaming and vocalizing your stream of consciousness.

Honor the intentions and visions that await in your heart. To honor them—they must first be seen.
—mar

If the visions just won't begin, here are a few ideas to get the process started: You just took office as the president of the United States—what changes do you make first? Your daughter has just graduated from college and you are giving her some sage advice about the grand possibilities for the future—what do you say? You have just arrived in Heaven—what is your life like there?

Some dreams translate quite directly into intentions. A dream that I'm going to have my own company is an inspiration and can be an intention—a lot of our dreams are like that.

As another scenario, I want to find and marry someone who is wonderful, with whom I'm in love, and who has twelve specific characteristics. That is also probably an intention and actionable—depending on the characteristics I demand.

However, a lot of our dreams don't translate well into being intentions. These are dreams such as "I want to end illiteracy." To turn a dream like that into an actionable intention, ask questions. Ask more questions. Ask deeper questions. *Why* do you want to end illiteracy? *Where* do you want to focus? *Who* do you most want to help? Continuing to refine your dream, you eventually get to something that is actionable.

Perhaps you refined "end illiteracy" to "end illiteracy in America" and eventually to "tutor inner-city children." Or, perhaps you refined it to "end illiteracy in Africa" and then to "join the Peace Corps."

Then ask yourself two questions:

1. Does it still feel like my dream?
2. Am I willing to make the commitment?

"Tutor inner-city children" may not inspire you, or you may not be willing to make the commitment of joining the Peace Corps. Gaining that insight into your nature is actually a great outcome. You now know one more thing that is *not* your dream. That frees you to restart your dreaming. Have patience—the answers will come.

My dream does not have to be noble or self-sacrificing. It is just as valid for my dream to be "take early retirement and write my memoirs," as something like "end illiteracy worldwide." Whether I am seventy or twenty-seven, I can choose today to leave or stay at a job I hate. However, if I am twenty-seven, the choice to stay can turn into a prison sentence of suffering (rather than a dream): "I'll work hard at this job I hate for the next forty years, and then I'll retire and begin to enjoy life."

No dream is too big or too small, as long as it is truly inspiring. In 1920, my uncle Jimmy Yen made a vow to eradicate illiteracy in rural China. Within twenty years, tens of millions had learned to read because of Jimmy. On the other hand, turning one's woodworking or quilting into a career is no less valid. Dreams are completely personal—whatever is inspiring to you is right.

There *is* a dream inside each of us that screams every day, "I am your life! You can't ignore me!" If it doesn't scream at you every day, it's not the real dream. Have patience. Have compassion. Inspiration will come.

Once you find your dream—your passion—you know it. It owns you and cannot be denied. Whether your dream is joining the Peace Corp, entering politics, or writing your memoirs, once you can taste your dream, you can start taking action.

> When I can taste, smell, and touch my dream, I can enroll the world.
>
> —jlh

Once I have turned my dream into an intention, I can begin to look at who I can enroll into my dream. To enroll someone means to inspire them and gain their commitment. Enrolling somebody into my dream doesn't necessarily mean that I am going to direct their activities.

There are public dreams, like ending world illiteracy, and private dreams, like turning a hobby into a vocation. Once I launch a public dream, I am no longer its sole owner. Once I enroll other people, we are all enrolled. People are enrolled in the vision that I began—not in me as an individual. It is important that I not take personally anything that those who fell in love with my vision do or don't do.

> When the best leader's work is done, the people say, "We did it ourselves."
>
> —Lao Tzu

The ancient Chinese saying about the greatest leaders being invisible—the people think they have done the work themselves—that is what happens when people get enrolled into a cause.

Enrolling people into my vision is a bit different when it is a very personal vision. In that case, being enrolled means that someone is supporting me and cheering me on.

If my vision is living in Mexico, I am still going to want to enroll people into my vision. If I have a significant other, I certainly need to enroll her into my vision. Mexico would be a lot less fun if I was divorced and alone—unless that was my desire. If I have children, I would also want to enroll them into my vision—I'd like to have them come to see me sometime—or at least not disown me. The same holds for the rest of my family and friends.

The greatest power of enrollment comes when it allows my vision to eclipse the best future I had ever allowed myself to hope for. Perhaps my life plan had been to work hard for years and then to retire at fifty-five—a plan of suffering. I close my eyes and dream of living in that quiet, warm, friendly fishing village *today*, but try as I might, I can't see how I can make my finances work. What if I could enroll my employer in letting me telecommute—and move to Mexico now—with full salary? As a result of dreaming my future and enrolling others into my vision, I get to sit on my veranda, watch the waves, sip cheap margaritas, and telecommute.

If you now know your dream or have a sense of your dream, that's great. If you have no clue, that's great also. It may take days or years, so relax.

MAR If the process seems puzzling to you, try understanding your vision/purpose for your future by grasping the passions and enthusiasms of your past. Look behind you to when you were a child expressing those dreams which began, "When I grow up I'm going to . . ." Consider how your uncommitted time was spent. What pursuits that you chose voluntarily captivated your interest? Throughout my teenage years I wrote in large letters throughout my journals, "I want to be an artist." I knew from a young age that I was searching for the finest way to use my writing skills professionally.

I refresh my mission statement every few years just to make sure I'm connected and it still expresses the authentic desires of my heart. I will share two processes with you. In writing, I answer the question, "What is it that you want/ long for?" Here's my current answer:

INSPIRATION/SAIL

Unrelenting and profound creativity and creation
Vitality in spirit and body
Consciously incorporate my ten illuminating things into my day
Self-knowledge and self-awareness, which form the basis for guiding others

SUCCESS

Enjoy positive outcomes from appropriate investments
Redeem all actions and activities by observing and learning
Create an environment that supports my ontology and is consistent with what I want

INTIMACY

Invest in and develop my marriage
Demonstrate fearlessness and dedication in my friendships
Speak the truth with compassion
Act from love—face and dispel fears

RESPONSIBILITY

Fulfill the obligations that the past posts to me
Embrace the opportunity for service based in love

My mission statement has remained essentially the same for many years. I will share it with you:

Inspire and uplift myself and others;
Promote health, wellness through process and travel;
Become the finest version of myself;

Experience a book of mine with seventeen editions in
   my lifetime;
Participate in anonymous service and public citizenship;
Provide appropriate resources for my treasured circle;
Enjoy cherished, trusted intimacy.

CHARTING MY COURSE

JLH Eventually, I have my vision and see my future. It's rolling
through my head like a movie—full color, wide-screen, surround
sound—and yes, I can taste it and smell it. Now it's time to chart
my course.

I spent most of my career as a highly successful leader in Sili-
con Valley's go-go world of high technology. After a wild ride
through the inflated valuations of the late 1990s, I was able to
retire to travel and kick back. That was great for several years,
and then the visions began. First little snippets, and eventually
unstoppable full-color dreams that I could taste.

I had a mission. Sharing my vision of joyful living for all
through conscious choice began permeating my every fiber. I was
called. I was no longer calling my vision; my vision was calling
me, beckoning me, urging me onward—in spite of the illogic of
the enterprise. I had retired with enough money to live comfortably without working, and writing is hard work. Few authors even
make minimum wage—especially self-awareness authors. Try telling that to the vision. True visions don't work on logic—they are
compelling beyond all logic.

How do you know when your dream is "the one?" When your
dream runs through your head like a full-color movie, pleading
with you to take action.

Unfortunately, a compelling dream is just the beginning. The
obstacles to fulfilling the dream, or even to launching it, are often

nearly overwhelming. Be prepared to meet these challenges and more:

- Most big dreams appear illogical and unattainable. Consider Jimmy Yen's dream to eradicate illiteracy in rural China—totally illogical and unattainable.
- Our friends and family *are* going to tell us that our big dreams are crazy and that we should settle for less.
- Usually, we have to stop doing something else in order to make room for our big dream. I had it easy, but usually people have to give up one career to begin another, or have to essentially work two jobs at once—the one that pays the bills today, and the one they truly love, which may not pay off for years.
- We are unable to anticipate what the future will bring and what consequences may result from taking action on our dreams.

So, what will you do? Will you chart the best course you are able, given the information you have access to today, and set sail? Or will you trash your dreams into the box labeled Fantasy Discard Pile and return to doing what others expect of you?

Stand tall, breathe deep, and choose today to chart the course that will transform your dream into reality.
—jlh

MAR Once you have established your course, or identified your life mission, it becomes the natural tool against which all opportunities are measured. Understanding your vision works just like a yardstick. It creates a set of questions you can ask about anything you are considering investing your time and personal skills in. I have a set of measures I consistently apply based on my own vision for myself.

I ask:

- Do I have available time, interest, and ability?
- Is this consistent with my vision for my life and what I want?
- Will this help me become a finer version of myself?
- Will this create resources for my circle of friends and family?
- Does it express service or citizenship?
- Does it promote friendship and/or intimacy?

Try creating your own set of measures once you are connected to your vision. One of the most valuable outcomes of these questions is the clarity and strength to say *no, thank you* more frequently to opportunities that do not match my mission and *yes* to those that have a significant impact.

INTENTION: DREAM BECOMING REALITY

Every thought we think is creating our future.
—Louise L. Hay

JLH In everyday speech, my intent, or my intention, is my plan and desire to move toward a goal or target. "I intend to go to the store this afternoon." It's just my plan and desire, nothing more. Is my intent ever anything more than that?

What I intend with compassion and without ego has a remarkable pattern of showing up. Illnesses heal. Pains vanish. Answers appear. Amazingly loving and supportive people show up in my life. When I intend for something to happen, the forces of the Universe align with my intention and miraculously transform my intention into reality *if* my intention is egoless and compassionate. Intent will not help in winning the lottery, but if I have an egoless intent for abundance, the Universe will create conditions in which I experience a sense of abundance.

The power of our intent is limitless. Always intend with conscious awareness and compassion.

My greatest power and inner peace come when I intend future events with compassion, and when I avoid assuming or expecting them. Contrast my intention with my assumption and my expectation that certain events will occur in the future. Intention couldn't be more different from assumption and expectation.

Intuition

Intuition . . . that sixth sense, that indescribable feeling of *knowing* something that objectively we do not know. Intuition tells us when our child needs our help or a business deal isn't as good as it appears.

Does intuition actually tap into a kind of universal life energy that science has yet to identify? Or is what we call intuition actually our brain processing available information, obscuring the computation process and intermediate results, and only informing us of its final conclusion? Whatever its explanation, intuition is immensely powerful.

Intuition, in the broadest sense, is not limited to humans. Consider the migrations of birds, fish, butterflies, and other animals. The arctic tern migrates twenty-four thousand miles every year—Arctic to Antarctic and back. After a twelve thousand-mile trip, the arctic tern arrives at exactly the same location as the previous year. Salmon return to exactly the same place in the river where they were born to breed and die there.

Scientists studying these migrations believe that the stars, the sun, the earth's magnetic field, winds, and some innate sense of the passage of time all contribute to birds' ability to migrate. They attribute salmons' migration mostly to their ability to "taste" the water in which they were born—even hundreds of miles at sea—and follow that taste back to its source.

Whether animal migration demonstrates access to an undiscovered living energy, or whether it can all be explained by celestial, geomagnetic, and other clues, I'm going to call it intuition.

The explanation for the phenomenon of intuition is far less relevant than our experience of intuition and the benefits that conscious use of intuition can bring to our lives. We can celebrate our intuition and utilize it to live more joyful lives.

Intuition and Intention

Intuition and intention are like a radio receiver and a radio transmitter. The signals being transmitted are ethereal, and not yet understood by science, a universal life energy that we share with all living things. Intuition is our receiver—we sense the life energy in which we are constantly bathed. Sometimes we don't pay any attention to our intuition. Sometimes we get confused and agitated by the presence of so many conflicting messages. Sometimes we receive a message loud and clear.

Intention is our transmitter of universal life energy. When we intend for something to happen, we transmit that message to all life. Sometimes we transmit a confused or weak message. Sometimes we transmit a strong, clear message. Sometimes our message is received. Sometimes it isn't.

Most of us are much better transmitters than receivers. Imagine that you are traveling to a foreign country as a tourist. You pick up a phrase book with the intention of becoming able to communicate, at some rudimentary level, with the locals. What happens?

Speaking is the easy part. It's pretty easy to master saying "Where is the toilet?" and be understood. The hard part is understanding the answer. Pretty soon, you figure out that the way to understand the answer is to ask questions that can be answered with yes or no, or by pointing. "Would you please point toward the nearest toilet?"

In a similar way, while training our intuitive skills, it works better to ask questions that have yes/no answers. Pendulums, muscle testing (applied kinesiology), and similar devices or procedures facilitate intuition by forcing their user to only ask questions that have yes/no answers. You can gain the same advantage simply by disciplining yourself to only ask yes/no questions of your intuition. As a simple example of a procedure to facilitate intuition, try this exercise:

1. Choose a time when you are relaxed, your mind is calm, and you have access to a quiet room without interruption. Breathe deeply, and if possible, practice yoga or Qigong, to quiet your mind before you begin.

2. Sit comfortably with your back straight and your feet flat on the floor.

3. Close your eyes, and fully extend your arms in front of you. Attempt to keep each of your arms exactly horizontal.

4. Assign one of your hands to represent a yes answer and the other a no answer. The hand that is higher than the other after you open your eyes determines the answer.

5. Ask yourself a question that can be answered with a yes or no answer. Begin with a test question to which you know the answer, such as, "Is my name John Q. Public?"

6. Pause and repeat the question silently several times.

7. Open your eyes and discover how you have been holding your arms. It is likely that you will find that you are holding one of your hands higher that the other, possibly a surprising amount higher.

If you find that your body unconsciously delivers the correct answer to several test questions, you are ready to ask an important yes or no question, such as, "Should I quit my job?" Otherwise, try the process again at a time when your mind is calmer.

After you have become skilled in using an unconscious arm position, pendulum motion, or dowsing rod response to answer questions, you can begin to visualize the yes or no answer to your question without the use of a physical aid.

How does a technique such as this work? Some would say that a universal energetic force moves your arms. Others believe that techniques such as this simply provide a mechanism to access your own uncensored preferences. You may not be willing to say that you should quit your job, but you allow your body to speak for you. There is no objective scientific proof that such techniques work, as there is no scientific proof for the existence of intuition or intention, and many remain skeptical.

Returning to intention . . . Every one of us has the ability to transmit a message such as "I am relaxed and joyful," "My headache is easing, and I feel comfortable," or "My friend's tumor is shrinking rapidly," and have that message received by the Universe.

Power of My Word—I Choose My World

There is immense power in our speaking. When we compliment people, we raise their energy as well as their self-esteem. We also raise people's energy and self-esteem when we tell them that we love them and choose to be with them. This action also raises our own energy. On the other hand, when we gossip, we lower the energy level of everyone involved—ourselves, those we gossip to, and those we gossip about. This effect is greatly exaggerated if the gossip is also a lie—slander, false witness.

> *Use the power of your word in the direction of truth and love.*
>
> —don Miguel Ruiz

Often, we do not recognize and honor the power in our own speaking. When we stop paying attention, we just open our mouths and let a stream-of-consciousness flow out. On occasion, that works, but more frequently that kind of thinking contains unkindness, bias, or outright untruth—and then it's too late. Even if we immediately recognize the bile that has come from our lips, it is too late to take it back.

TODAY IN MY WORLD:

For everything you say or do today, ask yourself, "What is my intent? Is my intent pure?"

FOCUS PHRASE WRITING: PATHWAY TO NEW BEGINNINGS

MAR I will share a writing process with you that I've used for years. I first used it as a study tool when I was a teenager. It has increased my understanding, stretched my perspective, and introduced profound and fresh insight into my life. I've named this method "Focus Phrase." As a practice, it helps develop your ability to observe your world, both externally and internally. It is a process you can utilize once or for a short period of time. For the most dramatic impact, I recommend you write, consistently, for a full month.

This process is a lens through which we can view our daily life and gain differing perspectives. I'd like to share some success stories from folks who have followed the Focus Phrase process for at least a full month. From their shared experiences you may draw some conclusions that will be helpful for you.

> I have been doing focus phrasing classes with Mary Anne for a year now. It has given me a way to express myself through writing that I haven't been able to achieve before. I have found this process so beneficial that I am now doing focus phrasing with my clients to create clearer business visions for their companies. I can use anything to create Focus Phrases. I have a client that is starting a new magazine. After our initial meeting I sent him a Focus Phrase every day for a week and asked him to create his mission statement one day at a time. It was very successful. He said it took away that overwhelming feeling of trying to come up with it all at once. I have used focus phrasing to create holiday plans, my move to Colorado, daily journaling. Learning an expanded vocabulary. You can use focus phrasing for anything.
>
> —Sandra Allison

> The Focus Phrases illuminated my life. Each phrase shined a light into my thoughts. During the month-long experience, I contemplated making changes in my life and the phrases helped me weigh my choices. In the end, I decided to participate in a triathlon. The second time I participated, I examined how to enliven my holiday season as an empty nester. Instead of facing the season with dread, I embraced and welcomed the new opportunities and freedom. Ultimately, Mary Anne's thoughtful and provoking phrases wakened my thinking process, and helped shine a spotlight on my path.
>
> —Paula Rudberg Lowe

Focus Phrase is an opportunity to become clear about what matters in your life and to seek the courage to act on that. During the process of Focus Phrase writing—I've done it twice now—I listened to phrases with my heart and explored new ways of answering questions of the soul. I found a focus, that "still place in a turning world" as T.S. Elliot wrote, and it directed me to clarify my values and to take the actions that would further those goals. As I told Mary Anne, her Focus Phrases are cheaper than therapy and it only took three paragraphs a day!

—Jane Kirkpatrick

Take this opportunity and use it as a focus exercise for thirty days. This is where the focus begins. On purpose. It's dynamic. You are both the teacher and the student. The benefits are as varied as the events of your day. Some consistently identified outcomes are values clarification, personal behavioral insights, resolutions of ongoing issues, identification of specific goals, and motivation for achieving dreams.

There are a few key elements that are required for the process to be effective:

- Daily participation.
- Commitment to honesty in your writing.
- Freedom from judgment about the style of your writing.

Focus Phrase is about process and results. Writing is a tool, not necessarily the most significant outcome. Clarity and new perspectives are among the possible outcomes.

There are many phrases to choose from in the course of a month. I will offer some for your use. One approach is five days on with two days off. The break helps to sustain the momentum and keep you from becoming overworked. The alternative is writing every day for a month. Some report the continuity is important to their process. These pages have been designed for you to copy and create daily phrase cards . . . however many days you choose to use the method.

Begin with phrase one the evening before your first Focus Phrase day. Consider the phrase before you go to sleep. Be aware of it when you wake up. Write the phrase on a piece of paper and put it somewhere that you will see it throughout your day: in your wallet, in your planner book, taped to a cupboard door, on the side of your computer screen. Use the phrase as a lens to look at the events of your day. Use it as a frame of reference when you are considering options, having conversations or working on projects of any sort. Sometime near the close of your day, write no more than three short paragraphs regarding what stood out in the day. What did you notice, learn, shift, or ponder in relation to the phrase? Write these three paragraphs and then begin the process anew by reviewing the phrase for the following day before you go to sleep.

A writing partner specifically requested that I suggest forms in which the observations could be framed. Like a memo, a recipe, an invitation. Bonnie shares her experience as to why the structure worked better for her than simply just the instruction to write three short paragraphs.

Mary Anne's use of specific structures as part of the Focus Phrase process can be a critical element in the self-discovery process. Just as an archaeologist has specific tools and brushes to uncover ruins, the structures are tools to uncover thoughts buried deep within. The structure may help to trigger a lost memory, develop a wishful longing, deliver a long overdue message, or pass on helpful information. The structures become a part of a tool box to use as you go through the Focus Phrase process and become an enhancement for displaying and conveying your thoughts.

—Bonnie Hammersley

One of the significant impacts that people share with me is how important it is to them to know that someone is reading what they have written. It creates accountability for the practice. And it is also satisfying to reach out with words. You could ask a friend to partner with you in the process. Or perhaps there is someone in your world who wouldn't want to write daily but would be interested in being your reader and sharing thoughts with you about what you have written. Consider that as an option rather than just writing in isolation. Sharing discovery is both a real vulnerability and a satisfying gift. Here are some phrases of mine that you are welcome to use as Focus Phrases. You can draw your own phrases from scripture, poetry, or favorite quotes.

Simply an Inspired Life Focus Phrases
—mar

For yesterday I hold no apologies. For tomorrow I offer no answers.

What compass do you use to discover the direction of your possibilities?

Awaken to the contradiction that life only makes sense when I admit it makes no sense.

The past is wind at my back. It blew me here, but it does not govern me.

What is the *what* of what just happened? What is the *how* of how I will view it?

From which base am I operating—love or fear?

Where can I purchase a well-suited pause?

Consider the values of silence as an appropriate response.

Repetition is a natural breeding ground for expectation.

How do the unwritten and often undisclosed rules of my life impact my day?

The path to honoring myself is paved with my dreams, my intuitions, my longings, my special celebrations.

All of life is a matter of perspective, and I can bring to whatever task any attitude I wish.

Choose joy.

Right now I am investing the currency of my spirit in my own joy.

Don't take it personally—it's not usually about you.

Forgiveness lives in the present.

Forgiveness is willing to see a situation in the context of itself, rather than through a lens of being right or being wrong.

I tell the truth as I know it. That's all I can do.

I allow myself the freedom of vulnerability.

Gratitude is the light in the dark corners of each day.

I release myself from the choices and history of others. I do not condemn myself to the sorrows of another, nor do I bind myself by anyone else's expectations.

Even those things which seem out of reach of my choice are governed by how I choose to perceive them.

Vision stands on the shoulders of what is actual to get a better view of what is possible.

There is no waiting for a different kind of life. This life *is* your life: live it.

Celebration has many different outfits, but she always wears the same beautiful dancing shoes.

I can create a ceremony or ritual that makes sense to my own values, needs, and life experiences.

Joy is a choice.

I keep one eye on my priorities and the other eye on opportunity for joy.

Don't wait.

As we light a path for others, we naturally light our own way.

May gratitude be the fire in your belly.

At the end of your own Focus Phrase writing process, review what you have written. Notice if there are common themes or repetitive issues. Use it as a way to come to a deeper understanding of how you see your world. And, perhaps most significantly, it is an invitation to keep writing.

Transforming into Your Inspired Future

Being fully enrolled with an understanding of vision and purpose is an invigorating place to be. It invites you to begin each day as if it were on purpose . . . because it is. From such a perspective, so many things feel possible. Here's the greatest news—they don't just *feel* possible, they *are.*

Chapter 8

ACTION—With Bold Courage

AFFIRMATION I Act with Bold Courage—Taking inspiration from the powerful vision of my future, I boldly set sail with courage and intent. I hold my course with focused attention and relentless commitment, as I weather the storms of life. ॐ

The wise man in the storm prays God, not for safety from danger, but for deliverance from fear. It is the storm within which endangers him, not the storm without.

—Ralph Waldo Emerson

Choose with no regret.

—mar

I say yes to the opportunities life offers me.

—jlh

COURAGE DOESN'T ALWAYS ROAR

Sometimes courage is the quiet voice at the end of the day saying, "I will try again tomorrow."
—mar

MAR Long ago I picked up the notion that courage involved grand gestures and was rather loud. The deafening roar of a blazing fire demanding the courage of the fire professional who runs into burning buildings instead of out of them. A lion with that earth-trembling roar that announces, "Here is the king." A soldier. The overwhelming *whoosh* of an Olympic competitor rising from a fall.

I began seeing courage in different terms . . . with the volume turned down when, over twenty years ago, a good friend came to me in tears. The requirements on her as an adoptive mom were overwhelming. The needs that her precious daughter brought with her from another country were a puzzle missing many pieces. I wrote a poem for her that began, "Sometimes there aren't any trumpets . . . just lots of dragons." The piece of comfort for my friend became, in time, the rewritten piece that forms this headline.

This aphorism has comforted me on some spectacularly discouraging days. Called me when I wavered close to giving up. I would hear, "Courage doesn't always roar . . ." and it made me realize that my tomorrow would give me another opportunity. Sometimes just an insight, or seeing the truth, constitutes the real roar of courage. More than any other phrase I have written, this walks with me as my teacher and cheerleader. I have come to understand that it is true for other people as well.

Sometimes courage expresses itself by simply acting on instinct and reaching out to someone. Not necessarily reaching through fire, but reaching nonetheless. An executive who kept a small stash of my writings in her desk "for special occasions" stepped into my store one day and shared an amazing account of this phrase with me.

A coworker had seemed out of sorts for a few days. She wasn't close to him and didn't feel comfortable asking if something was wrong, but before she left, she followed an impulse. She put a little card with the courage quote in the center of his desk.

What she learned early the following Monday was stunning. He returned to the office Saturday morning to put his office in order. He planned to take his life later that day. The message in the middle of his desk prompted his call to a suicide hotline where he started in with help and healing. As this woman was known for sharing my writings with folks, the man assumed correctly that she had left that card for him, and went to her the following week and told her his story.

A small gesture. A few words. A quiet whisper, really.

Set SAIL with Courage: To Act in the Face of Fear

JLH Acting in the face of fear isn't just about a fireman rushing into a burning building to save a child. Sometimes acting in the face of fear is just to get out of bed today. Every day we are afraid, and still, every new day awaits us . . . awaits our action, whatever that might be.

To act in the face of fear is, to some extent, about what actions we choose to take, but to a greater extent, it is about choosing to take action joyfully, boldly, and compassionately.

I am a human being—so I am afraid—it's that simple. All human beings are afraid from time to time—some more often than others—some more intensely than others. Fear is related to circumstance, but more so to our attitude and our degree of preparation. We can never be totally without fear, but we can learn to deal with our fear. The path to an Inspired Life is not without fear—rather, we walk that path by managing our fear, living with our fear, being at peace with our fear.

Adventure—A Paradox

Our deepest fear is . . . the unknown. One of our greatest longings is . . . adventure—our quest into the unknown. It's a paradox.

Why do humans long for adventure? Part of the answer is our curiosity. We want to discover answers. We want to create more of the known and less of the unknown in our world.

Perhaps the greatest part of our longing for adventure is our desire to play around the edges of our fear of the unknown, like a child playing near a fire, asking, "How close can I come without getting burned?"

A third part of our quest for adventure is our desire for recognition. That recognition comes in two forms. Adventurers, male and female, are often honored as brave and heroic, but it appears uniquely male for adventure to be a sexual display—like a peacock flaunting his plumage. "Oh, you big strong man. You slayed the dragon and returned with that magnificent scar on your cheek." Those words would drive many a man to cross Arctic wastelands or to venture into battle.

When you think of adventurers, who comes to mind first? For me, they're Amelia Earhart, Admiral Robert Peary, and Charles

Lindberg. Does it matter that all were passionate publicity hounds? Does it matter that Earhart and Peary took reckless chances? Does it matter that Peary's claims of North Pole discovery are now generally doubted? These people would never have gotten financial backing for their adventures—let alone be remembered by us—if they hadn't been such ardent self-promoters. They are the leading fringe of adventurers.

For the rest of us, adventure is something to be undertaken in moderation. It's clear why we might want to avoid adventure—it's scary, and often it's dangerous. So why adventure at all? Life is dull and uninspiring without adventure. Adventure is the spice of life. We can live just fine on nice, healthy, reliable oatmeal, but oatmeal just doesn't compare with an occasional feast of curry or chili—even with the penalty of a little heartburn.

For most of us, adventure has some element of honor-seeking—especially for young men hoping to flaunt their bravery to misty-eyed damsels—and some element of curiosity, but our primary reason is metaphorically playing with fire—tasting a sense of danger—whether real or imagined. Roller coasters are so popular because they let us feel the fear and the satisfaction of overcoming it without actual danger.

TODAY IN MY WORLD:

Make a list of times you have chosen to engage in dangerous or frightening activities. Note those times for which there was a useful purpose and you acted with bold courage—such as being a firefighter and entering a burning building. For the other times, write down why you took the risk. Are there times that you can see that you engaged in the dangerous activity in order to impress a member of the opposite sex, or to defeat a rival? Times you quested for knowledge? Times you adventured just to play with fire?

Making Bold Actions by Using What You're Good At

MAR One hundred thousand. One hundred thousand of anything sounds like a lot. The average American will work one hundred thousand hours during a lifetime. Doing what you enjoy is invigorating and makes moments move quickly. Think about the one hundred thousand hours you may spend in your lifetime working and how much greater the reward would be if you weren't just clocking time but rather finding ways to make bold, courageous actions with what you're good at.

For some, the workplace is in their home. For others it is an establishment away from home. There are still others who spend so much time in their workplace that they joke they ought to call it home. In any case, it's work. Are you one of those people who view the workplace (or the school you attend) as just marking time in order to get to the real and enjoyable, personal parts of your life? Is it what you do every day in order to earn time to do what really matters? You can change that by making good with what you're good at.

Many people consider their personal skills and passions just that—personal and off limits at work. Some wish they could apply their most enjoyable activities at work but don't see how they translate.

I worked as a personnel department secretary in a large manufacturing plant. I was tied to my desk with predictable tasks. At home I spent a lot of time sending cards, making signs and artwork, creating events and celebrations for my friends, and finding little generosities to share with people to let them know I cared.

The personnel department had a formula for honoring the individuals who were retiring. Everyone received exactly the same things. Same cake. Same logo-engraved pen set.

I saw an opportunity to make good with what I was good at. I put together some suggestions that utilized my personal talents and benefited the company. They liked it! Ultimately, I was able to interview the retirees months in advance and learn about their dreams and hopes for retirement. In addition to company logo-imprinted products, they received thoughtful gifts that pertained to what they hoped to do in their retirement. I lettered signs and cards. I made sure the cake was their favorite flavor, decorated with something meaningful to them. Small things which contributed to a large memory for everyone. I enjoyed it, and it dramatically improved my work experience.

Your personal interests don't seem immediately transferable to the workplace? Ask yourself, "What are the process or results involved in my personal interests that might translate to the workplace?"

In examining the bold, courageous actions that you're good at:

- Be clear on the personal things that you are good at *and* that energize you. Look for direct, indirect, or imaginative ways you can apply them at work.

- Lay out your vision with a proposal: get your supervisor's approval.

- Implement your idea.

- Involve others, with the chance to make good with what *they're* good at . . . and inspire them with your courageous actions.

One hundred thousand hours just got more invigorating and rewarding. And inspired.

LIFE DOESN'T PLAY FAIR—BE PREPARED AND STAY FLEXIBLE

> *Welcome the conquering hero—and recognize that the hero is . . . you.*
>
> —jlh

JLH   The greatest battle of all is simply life. This is no child's game. This is the big one—the Super Bowl—the game of all games. The rules of life are unwritten and unknown. Perhaps, one could say there are no rules. The Judge has ultimate power—She can call the game at any time, for any reason. The penalties in the game are completely arbitrary—in both timing and severity.

"Penalty for what?" we ask.

The Judge is silent.

"How can I win the game?"

"You can never win," comes the answer. "So just take pleasure in playing the game."

Training—Wax On, Wax Off

> *First, wash all car. Then wax. . . . Wax on, right hand. Wax off, left hand. Wax on, wax off . . . Don't forget to breathe, very important.*
>
> —Mr. Miyagi in *The Karate Kid*

Training is very different from teaching. Teaching is what happens in a physics class or an English class. Training is what a sports coach does. When you are being trained in golf, for example, you don't focus on learning the physics of action-reaction, and you don't focus on the history of the game of golf. Rather, you are trained by your coach positioning your body, guiding your swing, and watching over you as you hit bucket after bucket after bucket of practice balls until your body bypasses your mind, your great swing feels natural every time, and whenever you sleep, your dreams are of hitting golf balls.

Training often doesn't make sense to the participant. Think of the football coach who insists his players run wind sprints for two weeks before they even see a football, or the great wax-on, wax-off scene from the 1984 movie *The Karate Kid* in which Mr. Miyagi trains Daniel in hand strength and coordination by waxing Miyagi's cars. Like the karate kid, we can best be trained by trusting the trainer and just accepting each day's training. The Not Doings training which follows is an example of the kind of exercise which holds far more power when undertaken with trust than after an attempt at intellectual analysis.

Not Doings—A Training

There is great power to the practice of occasionally doing exactly the opposite of what we are in the habit of doing. This practice occurs in several ancient wisdoms, including Taoist and Zen Buddhist traditions. I love the name Not Doings—which comes from the Toltec tradition and was introduced by Carlos Castaneda.

In a most wonderful book with the unfortunate title of *The Complete Idiot's Guide to Toltec Wisdom*, my good friend Sheri Rosenthal describes Not Doings as: "activities designed to put our doings in the spotlight and make them obvious to us, so that we can change them." One of the simple yet powerful examples she uses is having introverts and extroverts swap roles for a day. A chatterbox would maintain silence, while someone shy would intentionally step out to tell jokes and stories. I experienced this exercise firsthand on a spiritual journey to Guatemala led by Sheri. As I am by nature very quiet in groups, Sheri asked me, as a Not Doing exercise, to prepare five jokes and tell them to the group that evening. My first instinct was to refuse. I didn't *want* to tell jokes. I didn't want to embarrass myself. I didn't want to look inferior to those of our group who were practiced extroverts.

But I didn't refuse, because I trusted Sheri as a coach. I didn't give in to my instincts or to the prattling arguments of my monkey mind. My jokes would certainly not have made the David Letterman show, but I survived, had a good time, and gained an appreciation of my ability to do what doesn't come naturally. I also gained an appreciation of the discomfort some of my fellow travelers suffered when they accepted Sheri's coaching to restrain themselves from compulsive talking, and the insights they also received from trusting the coach and completing the exercise.

TODAY IN MY WORLD:

Write down a quality that you believe defines your being—something that is so central to who you see yourself as being that you can't imagine being otherwise. Are you shy, funny, devoutly religious, a non-believer, an early riser, a night owl, a vegetarian, a carnivore, a sharp dresser, or a comfortable dresser? Do you wear glamorous makeup, or no makeup? Are you punctual, or do you have a casual relationship with time?

Pick a defining quality—either from the list above, or better yet, the first one that pops into your head—then consciously and consistently do exactly the *opposite* for the next twenty-four hours. For example, if you think you're shy, tell ten jokes today. If you are usually carefully made up, wear absolutely no makeup today.

Make note of how it felt to act opposite to your habitual way of being. What are your thoughts? How are your body sensations? Were you tempted to refuse to do this exercise? How did it feel to have the courage to trust the trainer and complete this exercise in spite of your discomfort?

Boldly Courageous Actions Cultivated Intentionally (And Remembering People's Names While You're at It)

MAR You've considered exploring courageous actions by doing the opposite of what you are comfortable with. Now here is a different way to explore. Have you grown up with the impression that the person you are by a certain age is pretty much who you are stuck being? Even Popeye sang out from the cartoons, "I yam what I yam . . . and that's all I yam." Contrary to that, and even though it has long been said it cannot be done, the hope of teaching an old dog new tricks is popping up all over the place. Self-help authors are encouraging you to change your life simply by transforming your thoughts. The cultural anthropologist Mary Catherine Bateson said, "We are not what we know but what we are willing to learn."

Throughout decades, I've cultivated the qualities I've needed to change my life. The fact that I don't know something, or that I'm not naturally skilled at something, rarely stops me from exploring it and trying it out.

A. A. Milne's Tigger is a wonderful model for cultivating the qualities that can change your life. In situations unknown to the enthusiastic Tigger, he declares *that* very unknown thing is "what Tiggers do best!" Tigger proceeds to give that activity his undivided attention. You could say he focuses with bold courage . . . frequently with good results.

We can learn accidentally. We can learn purposely. Learning comes in many different ways. There's a world of information and media at our fingertips. This lesson is about being willing to learn. Willingness comes from deep within.

Are there people in your life whom you especially admire? How many times over the years have you whispered, "Oh, she's so _____ (fill in the blank), and I wish I could be more like her"? The real question is, "Are you *willing* to be more like her?" If your answer is yes, then let me share some ways you can.

Consider the qualities you would like to cultivate in your life. Inadvertently you may identify them, in a negative way, every day. Can you hear yourself saying, "Oh, I'm terrible at remembering names"? By negatively identifying this trait, you are actually reinforcing the opposite of a quality you would like to cultivate. After you identify the quality you want to cultivate, look for people who model that quality. You can discover a model in your immediate circle, in a biography, in a current popular figure or celebrity.

I was seventeen years old, just beginning to expand my social network outside my school experience. I regularly assessed that I was awful at remembering people's names. I really was. My minister, Reverend Don Baker, served as senior minister to a congregation of thousands. I observed Pastor Baker in countless settings speaking to numerous people—and he always addressed them by name.

The second time he ever saw me, he addressed me by name—I was shocked and touched that among thousands of people, he cared enough about me to remember who I was. It gave me a real sense that he thought I was important.

In that same way, I wanted to demonstrate to people I met that I cared about them. I set up an appointment to meet with Pastor Baker, and I asked him two things, "How is it you remember so many people's names? And is it something you can teach me?"

I'll tell you what he told me. I started practicing it immediately. I started to cultivate a quality that changed my life: I learned there are six steps to remembering someone's name.

It is important to connect, however briefly, with that person. Focus only on her even if it is only for thirty seconds.

Say their name as many times as you naturally can. Repetition is the second key. For example, "Oh, Mary Anne. It is so nice to meet you. Is that Mary Anne without an *e* or . . . Oh, Mary Anne, *with* an *e* . . . just like Anne of Green Gables when she declares, 'My name is Anne . . . Anne with an *e*.'" That's the third key: associating their name with something already familiar to you.

As you are meeting her, touch her in some way. Shake hands with one or two hands, touch her shoulder or elbow, whatever is appropriate. Reaching out is the fourth key.

Use association and repetition if someone else has just introduced you to her. Thank the person for introducing her to you with something like this, "Jennifer, I want to thank you for introducing me to Mary Anne. And, Mary Anne, I know that if you are a friend of Jennifer's, we'll always have something interesting to talk about because Jennifer is a fascinating individual."

Pastor Baker said the fifth key was that it's important to practice—all the time with everyone. He suggested if I found the process challenging, I could ask for help from the very people whose names I was trying to remember.

Ask for help . . . the sixth key. I could say, "I am working on remembering your name because I think you're a person worth remembering. Will you help me the next time we see each other by reminding me of your name?"

Those were his six keys to remembering someone's name. I've added a seventh: the Tigger factor. Act as if you are already good at it. Stop asserting what you cannot do but rather assert that you *are* good at remembering people's names. In fact, remembering names is what you do best. And if you can't work your way up to the Tigger factor, then simply acknowledge, "I am practicing excellence at remembering people's names."

It took a few years, but by the time I was in my early twenties, I had cultivated the caring quality of remembering people's names. I remembered the names of folks I encountered briefly and wasn't sure I would ever see again. I knew I'd mastered the quality when people began saying to me, "I wish I was more like you. I'm no good at remembering names, not like you. You can remember everyone's names. It just comes naturally to you." Ha! Naturally after years of practice! Turns out I became a model of the very quality that I did not first possess. Not only was I able to demonstrate that caring quality that I wanted to take on, but this quality did change my life. People often told me in business that they were favorably impressed when I remembered them after meeting them briefly, once. It made them feel as if they really mattered to me. And they did, and do!

This story of learning to remember names demonstrates, contrary to Popeye's claim, that it's possible to be different tomorrow than we are today.

Think of a quality you would like to cultivate or a courageous action you would like to take. Perspective. Forgiveness. Change careers. Move to a different city. Then look for a model of this desired quality in your circle of friends, family, and acquaintances; look to a public figure who demonstrates this quality. Beyond that you can use the library, bookstore, or the Internet. A quick Internet search of "career change" yields hundreds of sites with a variety of suggestions. Focus on emulating the desired trait as this model person does.

> **TODAY IN MY WORLD:**
>
> There are a number of ways to learn to cultivate a new quality or to demonstrate a bold action. Try some of the following processes:
>
> Look up the definition.
>
> Find out what others have to say about it.

> Craft a phrase that summarizes what you have in mind.
> Tell a story about it.
> Write about an experience you've had with it or have heard
> about it.
> Discuss it with a good friend.
> Create practical ideas to boldly cultivate this quality in
> your life.

When you begin boldly cultivating courageous actions, you can tell all the Popeyes in your experience that you may be just what you are today . . . but tomorrow you'll be cultivating a quality or doing something that will change your life. And you can also say, "Because that's what I do best!"

Be Prepared

> *"Be prepared."*
> *"Be prepared—for what?"*
> *"Why, for any old thing!"*
>
> —Robert Baden-Powell

JLH For Robert Baden-Powell, the founder of Scouting, the motto "Be prepared" meant more than just being ready for emergencies. It meant being ready for all challenges to mind and body—meeting all of life's struggles with courage, happily and without regret, having done your best.

Pretty smart, those scouts. The motto of the Boy Scouts could be a way of life for all of us.

I first met Mary Anne in the Tampa airport as she flew in for a visit with her dear friend, my then fiancée, now wife, Suze. The first words out of Mary Anne's mouth were, "I need to get to a drug store for some Benadryl." She was suffering from a severe food allergy and had run out of the life-saving pink pills. As Suze prepared to hustle us off in search of a pharmacy, I opened my wallet and handed Mary Anne two Benadryl. They had been in my wallet unused—except for replacement as their expiration dates neared—for years, just waiting for that day.

Stocking medical supplies is the least of what it means to be prepared. Being emotionally prepared for the unexpected has even more value in helping us lead a joyful life.

When we use the expression "the unexpected," we are actually deceiving ourselves, for we know that people do lose jobs, become victims of crime, get sick or injured, and die. All that is unknown is the timing and details. For example, your neighbor ends his life with a gun, and you feel devastated and helpless. Is this event tragic? Very much so. But is it truly unexpected? Yes and no. That this particular man would choose to end his life in this particular way on this particular day is unexpected. That someone we know personally will end their own life at some time is a predictably likely occurrence. That friends and family whom we love and cherish will die is a certainty.

Just as we can stock Band-Aids and Benadryl, we can stock courage and fortitude in preparation for the unexpected tragedies—and celebrations—that *will* come our way.

Hoarding

We have come to view hoarding as something reprehensible and perhaps sinful, but we probably wouldn't be here today if our distant ancestors hadn't been accomplished hoarders.

Life's always had its ups and downs, and creatures, including humans, that prepared for lean times were the ones who survived—at least before our modern era of supermarkets and obesity. Like squirrels burying nuts and bears layering up with fat for the winter, humans have a long history of squirreling away, as it were, a readily accessible supply of calories—both around their own middles, and in secret or semi-secret hiding places—to be defended to the death against other human interlopers.

While it was essential for survival in times past, today hoarding has become the shadow side of being prepared. Obesity, materialism, greed, jealousy, and envy are today's manifestations of hoarding carried to excess. Being prepared is courageous, but hoarding is not.

STAY THE COURSE—GATHER STRENGTH FROM THE STORM

Kites rise highest against the wind—not with it.
—Winston Churchill

We choose our destination. We chart our course. We fill our ship with provisions. We set sail. And then . . . Airplane pilots are said to describe endless boredom punctuated by moments of sheer terror. When we least expect, the fury of the storm hits us broadside, and the choice is to set ourselves upright and continue, or to give up. In the words of the Japanese proverb, "Fall seven times, stand up eight."

Rider of the Storm

In the desert beyond the fringes of Santa Fe, New Mexico, I received the title Rider of the Storm during a dream quest. A dream quest is a Native American ritual for reconnecting with one's ancestors and requesting their guidance in setting the intent for one's life path.

A dream quest extends throughout a whole night and is essentially a guided meditation assisted by sleep deprivation and atonal, arrhythmic music. The shaman orchestrating the dream quest (a pleasant middle-aged woman, in my case) leads the participant through suggestion, alternating invitations to dream and to wake, and invoking the spirits of the ancestors to join the ceremony.

On the night of my dream quest, there was a thunderstorm of great fury. The whole house shook with the concussion of the explosive sounds, and the darkened room alternated between radiant flashes and impenetrable blackness. The storm found its way into my dream, and in my vision I was riding the power of the storm like a modern day Pecos Bill—cowboy hat in hand, legs wrapped tightly around the funnel of the twister, cheering wildly, and shouting, "I gather strength from the storm!"

Since that night, the metaphor of gathering strength from the storm has been extremely powerful in my life. Powerful events generate powerful energies, and those energies, while unrefined, contain the raw fuel to power any mission I wish to undertake.

My job is to refine the immense raw energies of the storms of life and to power my life journey from these vast resources. For me, this has meshed perfectly with the alchemy of Qigong and its ability to refine undifferentiated raw energy, or even recycled "dirty" energy, into pristine "new" energy to power my journey.

You can become a rider of the storm too. Whenever you become upset that life is not occurring as you planned, visualize your troubles as a wind storm. See yourself as Winston Churchill flying a kite high into the wind, or see Pecos Bill waving his hat and cheering, or see a SAILboat redirecting the wind to power its voyage. Better yet, create your own visualization that symbolizes gathering strength from life's storms.

> **TODAY IN MY WORLD:**
> Write about an experience that, while challenging at the time, increased your personal power in the long run.

Stir the pot

> *A life that is too comfortable has become stagnant. Stir things up. Call the storm. Provoke the wind. Challenge nature to a duel. Life is a game that can never be won, but is most enjoyable when played full out—boldly.*
> —jlh

LIVING INTO THE TWO GREAT PARADOXES

Much of life is paradoxical. We destroy our relationship when we smother our partner with loving attention. We fail to complete a project when we become enthralled by a drive to perfection.

Standing out among these smaller ironies, two great paradoxes dominate the nature of human existence.

Paradox #1

Having large goals for my life is key to my happiness—yet I will fail to achieve some of those goals, and I can only remain happy by avoiding attachment to my goals. A wise Little League coach might put it, "Play to win, but be a good loser."

Living a joyful and fulfilling life is a function of following our vision, rather than of achieving it. Yet, in paradoxical fashion, if we are not truly intent upon achieving our dreams, they lose their meaning.

The secret lies in following our dream with inspired intensity, while at the same time, gratefully accepting all the detours and new openings that life provides.

An inspired life lives not in the *doing*, but in the *being*. Whatever you do or don't do in your lifetime, your greatest contribution to your family, to your friends, to the world, and to future generations will be the happiness and joy you generated and radiated to others.

Affirmation

I travel my joyous and rewarding lifetime journey by generating a vision of my desired future, and then balancing the dual objectives of addressing all my energies toward my intended goals, while simultaneously experiencing satisfaction and joy in the face of whatever outcome actually occurs.

Paradox #2

I intend to be of the greatest service to the world, yet I also intend to honor the beliefs of others. Often I find conflict between these intentions. I am troubled as I remember the story of the anemic toddler with the parent who believed that a blood transfusion was a certain ticket to Hell.

Not all important questions have acceptable answers. Paradox #2 is the proverbial catch-22 or no-win situation. When there is no solution, what is there to do? Our wise Little League coach would probably say, "Just do your best." I would like to up the ante and say, "Have compassion, and just do your best."

Compassion toward self and others is the cornerstone of an inspired life.

—jlh

My overarching value is compassion. My intention is always to take whatever action or nonaction appears to be the most compassionate. I acknowledge that what appears to me to be most compassionate may not seem so to others, and that there is no absolute standard. In addition, I will consistently love and honor both myself and all others with whom I interact, and I will honor everyone's value systems to the extent that doing so does not compromise my compassionate actions toward others.

Now here is the paradox. There are times when it is impossible to do what I believe to be moral and simultaneously to act as other people's value systems demand.

When forced to choose between my personal sense of morality and honoring the value systems of others, my own choice is to proactively take actions or nonactions that uphold my moral code—even at the expense of violating someone else's value system. As an example, if I were a judge hearing the case, I would order a transfusion for the toddler—in spite of my great reluctance to violate anyone's belief system.

Each of us just does the best we can do. And through it all, we try to have compassion for everyone involved. I can feel compassion toward someone even when their value system violates my value system. I can have compassion for the parent of the anemic toddler even as I am providing a blood transfusion for his daughter against his wishes. The most important part of dealing with any no-win situation is universal compassion.

Paradox #2 is the cause of most wars. Sometimes war has other causes, such as greed or ego, but usually war is the result of each side believing that it is right and valuing its own sense of morality more highly than it values upholding the belief system of the other party. In the preceding paragraph, I just voted for war by declaring that I knew what was good for the young girl better than her own father did. But I honored my own value system.

Affirmation

I act to bring about my vision of the future, which is
based on my value system of what is right, just, noble,

compassionate, generous, humane, peaceful, and loving. Simultaneously, I accept that my vision is based on only my opinions and prejudices, and I honor all points of view and value systems, no matter how different from my own.

Remember that honoring the value systems of others does not necessarily mean not preempting them, possibly by force—such as when the other's value system condones torture or in the previous anemic toddler example. Have the courage to choose your own path as you traverse the maze of contradictions inherent in simultaneously honoring both your own convictions and your compassion for all.

The Loud and Messy Life

Get lost: that's how you find yourself.
—mar

MAR Some time ago I had an a-ha moment as I was talking to Jonathan about longings and fantasies about my writing life that didn't involve a bazillion different commitments and a variety of obligations and several places to be in a single day, and then—the a-ha. The realization dawned that while I've been waiting for this writing life, I have actually been leading a writing life. I've written an enormous body of work as I waited for my quiet, ordered practically Zenified writing life to arrive. Yes. I asked the question, "What if *this* is my writing life?"

I was in another conversation one day about so many things—failing health, right practice and rituals for healing, and how sickness still spreads, the factor of chaos, the component of the unknown, the mystery that escapes our liturgy and incantation. Or perhaps the mystery envelops our private practice so well we can't see the presence or the meaning of it.

I fell exhausted across our bed, and my husband said, "I'm sorry you have to write in a life like this."

I told him Anne Patchett wrote her first novel working double waitress shifts. I told him lots of other stories about amazing authors, and he stopped me. "I'm not talking about other writers' lives. I'm talking about yours."

That's when I remembered the time when I caught the glimpse that maybe Robert Frost's and Carl Sandburg's long daily solitary walks weren't going to be part of my writing life. I related my conversations in regard to the unexpected, the unexplainable, the chaos, ending with, "I've come to see that my writing practice occurs in the midst of this loud and messy life. The loud and messy life is what I learn my quiet from. It's where I get my lesson and gain my wisdom."

"That's a novel idea. Or a least a title."

I paused for effect and said dramatically, "I am uncertain I would be able to write a novel in such a loud and messy life." I laughed uproariously, relieved that I didn't wait all my life for my life to begin. Sometimes the things we really want silently sneak in our back door when we are looking elsewhere. Note to self: Notice.

Most of the people I know actually live fairly loud and messy lives. They discuss, as I did up until a while ago, the life they are waiting for. The more loving life. The more nutritional life. The more active life. The more abundant life. The life that has no dust under the bed and the books are in descending order on the bookshelf. The life for which they long every time they are at the checkout counter and see a magazine cover of *another* Martha Stewart publication. Ohhhhh . . .

The loud and messy life talks about balance in a different way—different from a perfect camera shoot for a magazine cover. One where passion is the balance to the mundane, where the have-to-dos are paired in some proportion to the want-to-dos. Because . . . life is precious.

I was with my dad as he was dying. He did not ever say he wished he would have worked more. As he died an undignified extinguishing death from Alzheimer's disease, he did not once express pride that he had never called in sick to work. No. He told me he was sorry he didn't spend more time with the family. That he didn't buy a few more things on credit so our lives would have been easier. He told me that by the time he knew what was important, it was too late for it to matter.

The loud and messy life reminds people that dirty dishes are not as big a deal as not investing in your community. That dog hair in the corner never killed anybody, but harshness, judgments, and lack of kindness kill a joyful heart.

The loud and messy life celebrates not knowing. Holding a friend's hand and just crying with snot running over your lips because you don't know how to pray for them.

It challenges people to cry out, "WIMIN?" What Is Most Important Now? This now. Not the now I'm hoping to buy for myself with my personal mantra, my aerobics class, and my nonfat yogurt with oat bran for breakfast. This loud and messy now, where ducks don't line up in rows, and prayers aren't (seemingly) answered, and the flame blows out of our ritual remembrance candles because we forgot to shut the window. This now.

Ask: What is most important? What will last? What will impact the hearts that matter?

What if this is the life I get? What if it really looks like the laundry piled on the corner of the sofa? What if my towels will never match? What if I learned to live to the edge of my passion and invested myself so deeply in the actions I intend for this day that I practically spit? That would be messy, wouldn't it?

Getting lost. The best way to find yourself, the boldest and most courageous action in a day.

Chapter 9

CELEBRATION—With Joy

AFFIRMATION I Dance with a Light Heart—I play with life, laugh with life, dance lightly with life, and smile at the riddles of life, knowing that life's only true lessons are writ small in the margin. ঌ

There are only two ways to live your life. One is as though nothing is a miracle. The other is as though everything is a miracle.

—Albert Einstein

Celebration has many different outfits, but she always wears the same beautiful dancing shoes.

—mar

The beauty does not live out there—the beauty's in my eyes.

—jlh

MAR Celebration is as much a way of looking at the events and experiences of life as it is an occasion marked on a calendar. In the process of celebrating the milestones of my life, both large and small, I have developed a bit of a reputation as a traveling party. Ha! I celebrate that reputation! A celebration is an opportunity to pass around the chance to honor and be honored. The pause to take note of a significant action, gesture, or accomplishment. As my father aged, he liked to say that just putting both feet on the floor in the morning was a reason to celebrate. From simple to grandiose, ordinary to beyond expectation, any day contains a host of reasons to create a celebration.

JLH In addition to sharing the same birthday—June 28—Mary Anne and I share the habit of traveling with well-stocked rescue kits. Mine tends toward Band-Aids and various patent medicines. Mary Anne's rescue kit favors everything needed for an instant celebration. She travels with a veritable party-in-a-package, or perhaps I should say that she *is* a party-in-a-package.

Mary Anne traveled to a friend's wedding in Oregon with her kit even more overflowing than usual. Gold spray paint, hair spray, lace, and an abundance of whatever joined the basics. She related pure delight at having a black buffing pad for the groomsmen's shoes—which had all gathered a fair share of dust.

At all times, Mary Anne is fully prepared to present a carefully wrapped, thoughtful gift for an unannounced birthday, an engagement or new job that begs for celebration, or just an unhappy day that needs cheering. Every gift from Mary Anne's celebration bag appears to have been painstakingly shopped for and uniquely wrapped especially for its recipient, even though Mary Anne may have just reached into her secret stash of hidden birthday loot or time-of-challenge mementos only moments before. This is her joy—for Mary Anne, celebrations are an essential part of life!

For me, celebration is a more personal ritual. In a sense, my whole life is a celebration. I celebrate nature. I celebrate beauty. I celebrate love, family, and friends. I celebrate that I am alive today. I celebrate my profound connection with Spirit and my unbounded gratitude for all of life.

WHAT *DO* THEY WANT?

MAR "What do you want for your birthday?"

"Oh, nothing. I have everything I need."

Ah. This exchange, repeated in various forms, over decades, makes knees tremble and strong, willful individuals whimper, "What *do* they want?"

Wanting. Questions. What do these have to do with celebration?

Celebration—noun, the action of marking one's pleasure at an important event or occasion by engaging in enjoyable, typically social, activity.

Celebration is a noun. It implies action. By definition, there's pleasure involved too. Well I'm going to do what I love doing—and that's bringing my own sense of value and meaning to a word. I'll share it with you.

The first thing I'll do to the standard definition is drop out "typically social." It's certainly a fine addition to any celebration, but not essential. When it comes to celebration, I'll be the first to confess that I enjoy celebrations and find reasons to have them almost any time at all. Sometimes, even though he's been dead for decades now, I can hear my dad's wry commentary over my shoulder. "Just getting out of bed in the morning and discovering my feet still reach the floor is a good enough reason to celebrate."

Well, yes. Indeed it is.

We are accustomed to celebrating events that commemorate significant things, often birthdays of all sorts (spiritual leaders, presidents and the like, all the way across the spectrum of celebrity to our close pals and our own birthdays). First times are birthdays in their own way—the first meal gathering of the Pilgrims and natives, the day the official Declaration of Independence was lettered. Last times are marked as well. The last day someone significant took a breath on the planet.

First times. Last times. Everyone has ways of marking and taking note of significant events. All over the world. Festivals. Carnivals. Unfettered partying. Tradition lays down footprints and expectation.

How do we bring the global into the personal? And what about that universally challenging question, "What do you want for your _____?" (fill in the title of the specific celebration here).

Whether you are noting a significant event, commemorating a particular action, or marking a first or a last or a dedicated commitment, the common factor in any of it is that you take note. You take note, observe, see. What do you see that has significance and merit? A pal of mine has dreaded her birthday for years. Who knows where these patterns start, but years ago things began going awry on her birthday and have had a nasty habit of lining up for birthday *bash*ing ever since. Events even conspired to rack up that memorable day the divorce is final on—yes, you guessed it—her birthday.

How can I celebrate with her? How can I not assent to the dreaded toll of what bad thing is going to happen this year? I'm certain that it is as we suggest—we see what we anticipate seeing. I do not want to anticipate with my friend that some distasteful fate will visit her birthday again this year. The most precious investment I am able to make in anything is my time. It is my highest valued commodity and the thing I cannot recuperate if I misappropriate it. I invested my time in the anticipation of my friend's birthday celebration. I sent a box to her that would greet her for the eight days leading to her birthday. Each day numbered with a card, a delightful phrase and a small gift. It was my contribution to sweeping out the cabin on her spirit and helping it welcome a good day, or at least a day upon which no terrible fate visits her.

A celebration requires that I see. Clearly. A celebration requires that I recognize the Golden Rule has no place in a celebration. The proverbial doing unto others as we would have them do unto us has done nothing to celebrations but give fodder for comedians and family arguments. That's how someone who does not golf gets golf clubs for Christmas and someone who does not really enjoy domestic pursuits gets a vacuum cleaner for a holiday. It is easy to give to others what we ourselves wish to receive. It's easy to create a celebration that we would enjoy having or participating in. The real key to a celebration is being attentive. Ah. Does this sound familiar? Because of course, attentiveness is clearly a key element in most aspects of a joyful life.

On the Fourth of July, I will enjoy a grilled hot dog smothered with mustard and a zesty potato salad as much as the next American. But there's something I do that I no longer try to impose on others—I re-read the Declaration of Independence. And I sit down with my copy of the Constitution and read it. Yes. Start to finish. And I thank the women who sacrificed the security of their households to say yes to a speculative revolution. I thank the family members who did not grasp the sleeves of the militia and those who took up arms and made it possible for me to (ultimately) vote in an American election. I express and honor the hardships and absence of comforts that the military faced. I thank shy George Washington for all the ways he was such a stand-up guy. And my friends who understand, who *see* me and the way I value celebrating this holiday, welcome my stories, my reflections. They indulge my leaning toward the serious on this festive day. They do it because they are attentive to my needs. And I—being attentive to the needs of my friends—no longer try (as I did when I was younger) to make them all sit down for a collective reading of the Bill of Rights. I have chosen components that are essential for my celebration. But I wisely do not impose them on others.

To celebrate is to create a memory that can be treasured by those all who participate. Celebration is a means to say to an individual who is being celebrated, "I see you. I recognize your uniqueness. I will take the time to understand you and will bring to this event my sense of *you* . . . not my sense of myself."

Celebration can be a spontaneous expression arising from a deep gratitude. It can be an attentive, planned, and purposeful effort to recognize the epistemology of another. It must be noted that even the best effort to see as another sees can fall short, due to that nasty little habit involving expectations. But certainly, from my own perspective, when I have committed my effort toward being attentive to another, I can celebrate (pardon the pun) my own finest endeavor.

The SAIL point of celebration, like all eight points, is not an isolated expression. It is tied intimately to gratitude, choice, and action. It is a grand partnership when those three work in concert with celebration. Attentively noting the firsts, the lasts, and the committed dedications of our lives as they come in large and small portions.

"What do you want for your birthday?"

"I want you to see me. I want you to attentively take note of me. I would like, even more than precious or well-selected things, to know that you have invested your precious time in my celebration."

Perhaps this answer whispers around the question of any celebration in our lives. I know Abigail Adams whispers to me across time and thanks me for remembering the days when she fed her family from virtually no resources while her husband was long away from Braintree serving the needs of not his young family but their young country. I know she and her neighbors appreciate the thoughtful, attentive remembering.

And I know my friend who dreads most birthdays will have at least a small spark of pleasure that her faraway friend stood apart from the anticipated dread and invested time in remembering joy. To celebrate . . . perhaps, then, is to partner choice, gratitude, and action and to celebrate the joys. Large and small.

CEREMONY AND RITUAL

In much the same way that I bring to the word *celebration* my own value and meanings, so we bring to celebration our own ways and habits. Over time, in the larger context of a culture, those ways become ceremony and the habits become ritual.

When I was in my mid-twenties, I was a single girl living in a smallish community. The greatest amount of my friends were paired and childed. They had holiday traditions unique to their family or families. For several years I'd felt like a fifth wheel in the holiday celebrations of kind families that included me—the lone single person in another family's Christmas. So I started a ceremony which turned into a tradition for many years. I created a grand Christmas morning celebration for those single folks in the community who, just like me, didn't want to spend Christmas morning alone, but neither did we want to be inserted as an odd one out in a celebration involving numbers of people we'd never even met.

Early in the season, we'd pick a gift theme. Something fun and affordable that would enable the whole crew of us to be gifted and gifting without busting our holiday bank. We took turns reading Dylan Thomas's *A Child's Christmas in Wales*. The experts at baking brought delectable cinnamon roles. Another brought the soundtrack for the morning. No one person was burdened with a lion's share of any responsibility. We all shared. Shared the time, cocreated the shared memories. And together we turned what could have been a dismal holiday into a festivity which we all looked forward to. We each took responsibility to re-create a tradition in the trappings which suited our lives and choices.

We can create ceremony and ritual that makes sense to our own values, needs, and life experiences. Borrowing from cultures that have practices which have evolved over hundreds if not thousands of years is grand as well. There are many traditional practices which we come to accept by default. Challenge yourself to consider what parts of a tradition—a habit—make good sense to you. And the parts that do not make sense? Jettison them. You choose.

JLH Celebration comes in many forms. We celebrate beginnings, transitions, and endings. We celebrate the special occasions of our lives, and we celebrate the anniversaries of those occasions. We all celebrate our happiest moments. Some of us are brave enough to celebrate all the major events in our lives. Is a funeral ceremony a celebration? It is if it's an Irish wake. Why wouldn't we celebrate a life well lived? Is the ninetieth birthday of a person with Alzheimer's a cause for celebration? How about the birth of a baby with Down Syndrome? All of life is cause for gratitude and celebration. Why not take every opportunity to celebrate? Why not just declare that the holiday of Today is reason enough to celebrate?

Rites of Passage

Rites of passage are the rituals that provide public acknowledgment of the joys and sorrows of the major transitions of our lives, such as birth, coming of age, marriage, and death. These rites of passage mark the end of one season of life and the beginning of the next, and have been celebrated from before recorded history:

Spring: Birth, and rituals such as baptism, begin the season of Childhood—the years of innocence.

Summer: Coming of age rituals such as confirmation or Bar Mitzvah mark the entrance into Early Adulthood—adolescence—the years of transformation when the caterpillar morphs into a butterfly.

Autumn: Marriage celebrates the beginning of the season of Middle Adulthood—the years of power, knowledge, and Family, when homes are built, families are raised, and the tribe is protected and fed.

Winter: Retirement marks the beginning of Late Adulthood—the years of wisdom and leadership, a time for focusing on teaching, leading, and ensuring the well-being of future generations. The end of the season, and of mortal life itself, is marked by the ritual of a funeral.

Notice that there are five transitions between seasons, but that only three or four are typically celebrated today. What about a celebration of the end of autumn and the beginning of winter? Perhaps that's the office retirement party, but if so, does it properly acknowledge the significance of the transition? And coming of age? A first communion or bar mitzvah is a gentle descendent of aggressive ancient traditions in which a boy might have risked his life to prove his worthiness to be called a man.

Perhaps, rites of passage would hold more power if they also memorialized each individual's personal life transitions, such as moving to a new community, leaving a marriage, or beginning a new career.

> **TODAY IN MY WORLD:**
>
> Consider each transition of your life and reflect on what was gained and what was lost. Was the transition honored by a rite of passage? If not, imagine how that transition would best have been celebrated. Would a celebration have supported you in creating a good ending that nurtured a strong and joyful new beginning?

MAR Wedding vows are a culturally significant rite of passage. There are time-honored sets of vows that can be used. More often individuals are personalizing the process by writing their own vows.

On a warm vernal equinox day, some years ago, tucked above the sea in a glorious many-windowed room, with an intimate collection of friends and family around us, the minister handed me the ring for my husband. He shared that the words we were about to speak were of our own making. As I put the ring on Mr. Gordon's finger, I declared my love and intent in this way:

> I now choose you to be my husband. To witness and assist in my becoming and allow me to assist in yours. To hold me, as your beloved, in your heart. I express gratitude for all the diverse events of my past, for they have all led me to stand by you. I give you my love, my steadfastness of purpose, and my will and my hope. It is my highest intention that we may always be, together or apart, unflinchingly who we are and to demonstrate an unwavering commitment to do what we are called to do. You are my true north. In our journey, I will depend on you for the read of our compass. I will honor you and adore you in every way for all the days of my life.

I wept as I gazed at this man of my dreams and spoke the words, "You are my true north."

Our minister handed my groom his ring for me. He declared his vows, having thoughtfully prepared in advance, with these words:

> This ring represents the joy which I will give to you that all your days may be strengthened. I choose you this day to be my "now." We begin writing the history of our lives together. All the paths of my life have walked me here to your side. In those paths I express my gratitude for all the ways which led me to you. I give you my best self. I'm honored that you bring your best self to me. I pledge to reach for the way which is truest and highest for us. I will live my days with the long prayer. We will continue to offer each other our most joyous selves.

Our guests saw our loving tears and understood we were speaking words from our hearts. I call to mind these vows as a standard and hold myself accountable to them.

> **TODAY IN MY WORLD:**
> Create unpressured moments to allow you and your partner to discuss the matters of your hearts. Ask important questions of each other. What is really important in your relationship? What do you believe will create a lifetime bond and what solemn promises can you make to uphold them? Distill your thoughts. Stick with the most significant things to each of you. Whether you are about to be wed or have been partnered for a long time, create a set of vows reflecting where you are in your relationship today. If you are single, use this process to develop an intention about the kind of relationship you would like to celebrate with someone else.

The Power of Naming

JLH When I renamed our cat Galena "Miss Piggy," it seemed cute, and I do love the Muppets, but it was a disservice to her and to myself. I started to see her ample curves with distaste. The name followed past reality, but it also called a future reality into being. Galena is now Galena again—named for the shiny gray mineral, the color of her beautiful fur.

Much of what we *are* is what we call ourselves, what we name ourselves. For years, I labeled myself shy, and I became more withdrawn and less comfortable around people. When I relabeled myself independent, my perception of myself and my world shifted.

From the day that I accepted the title Rider of the Storm, simply wearing that label has increased my personal power and altered my *being*. We *are* what we call ourselves.

MAR Two of my best girl friends and I were on our autumn retreat. One friend was in a very focused, intense period of time. The other kept having great blue herons walk up to her every time we went for a walk (how cool was that?). And me? You'll learn my phase of time in a minute. We were making jokes about needing to be superheroes in order to meet the variety of demands in our lives. One fit of laughter led to another, and before we knew it, we had superhero names: one was named for the elegant blue herons that kept following her around, my focused friend was dubbed Scrunchy Pants, and me? I was known for a while as Brainy Pants. They said it was because I loved research, and I had good ideas.

The superhero name quickly morphed into something less lofty. I became known as Bossy Pants, a title I deserved for the positive attribute of being able to manage crisis or difficult circumstances and help people come to efficient and effective decisions. And it was a title I deserved for a less than desirable attribute of offering to manage, in ordinary circumstances, others to come to my idea of efficient solutions. Over time, the superhero name I bore came to represent a quality which I genuinely wanted to change. And the name I bore did a disservice to me, just as the name Jonathan attributed to the cat was less than flattering. This title celebrated my actions which were less than honorable. I needed a change.

I paid attention to the way my superhero friend was assigned her lovely persona. The creature consistently came to her, showed itself to her. I reflected on the number of times I had been approached by eagles. I sat and discussed the significance of naming—the manner in which we call ourselves out from within—with my husband. We spent a lot of time exploring my mission, the nature of my goals, even my favorite colors and time of day. Upon reflection, I opted for a new superhero name, one that would call forward my finest inspiring qualities, not my worst bossy habit. That day I accepted a new name: Light Eagle. When I want to call up better behavior or a deeper level of courage, that is how I speak to myself.

TODAY IN MY WORLD:
THE NAMING CEREMONY:

Settle into a comfortable, quiet place. With eyes closed, contemplate who you choose to be. What is your costume? What is your persona? What is your new name, your new title? Write down all the candidate names that appear.

Relax and play with this. For example, if you're interested in gourmet cooking, try on Mistress of the Sharp Knife and Hot Flame.

Consider inviting some friends to suggest ideas, but remember that this is to be *your* name.

Be open and receptive . . . let the name choose you. When a name has chosen you, have a naming ceremony.

Choose a friend to share in this ceremony. Prepare a sacred space. Kneel before your friend, and have him or her place a hand on your head and say, "I name you _____. You *are* now _____." Stand up, look your friend directly in the eye, and say, "My name is now _____. I now *am* _____."

Whether you are now Keeper of the Flame, Soaring Eagle, Listener to Friends, Comforter of Animals, Gift to the World, or Happy to be Me, it is now who you *are*. Live into your new *being*.

At a broader level, ask yourself how you name others. Are there little nicknames that you call others that may be less than stellar or uplifting? How might you change that?

PERSONAL CELEBRATION

JLH When we think of celebration, most of us think first of Thanksgiving, the Fourth of July, New Year's Eve, and religious holidays. How about personal celebration? Is celebration inherently a group activity? Is it something we can do by ourselves? If so, what would we celebrate privately?

How we celebrate and what we celebrate are completely our own choice—as is whether we ever celebrate at all. I will propose that making personal celebration an ongoing part of our lives is an opportunity to greatly increase our joy, to give focus to our thanksgiving for life, and to renew our bond with Spirit.

How does personal celebration differ from gratitude? Gratitude is the silent prayer. Celebration is the outward expression of gratitude. Celebration—personal or communal—is the hymn and the dance.

Celebrating Rainbows and Butterflies

Rainbows and butterflies are themselves beautiful and highly symbolic, but they are also representative of all the small miracles of our life. My own rainbows and butterflies are the squirrels chasing each other around the apple tree, the deer and her fawn who visit us for the apples, the magnificent hawk who swoops low through our yard, the sea otters at play on the beach, the ungainly yet graceful and serene manatees that once came to swim with us.

Consider these metaphorical rainbows and butterflies:

- A gentle kiss
- A baby's smile
- The voice on the telephone that says, "I'm glad you called"
- The gentle whisper from the other side of the bed: "Sweet dreams. I love you."

- A song that touches your heart
- A bird in flight

TODAY IN MY WORLD:

What are your rainbows and butterflies? How often are you conscious of the small miracles that happen right before your eyes? How might your life be more joyful if you adopted a daily practice of celebrating your rainbows and butterflies? How might that celebration look?

Celebrating Sadness, Grief, and Overarching Courage

Sometimes, what there is to celebrate is our sadness, our grief, and our resolution to continue . . . courageously. We can then immerse ourselves in celebrating our acceptance of what is.

MAR Not all celebrations are based in whimsy. Some celebrations are remembrances of what was. Remembering. Essentially, remembering is at the core of many of our holidays. We remember the patriots who signed the Declaration of Independence. We remember the soldiers who dedicated their breath to serve our country. We remember the first meal the Pilgrims had with America's native inhabitants.

In loss, we remember a life that was once among us. Many people choose to call this a celebration of life rather than a funeral. In truth, death is one of the most reliable factors in our existence, and yet so often it manages to tap us by surprise.

Those who perceive eternity as a sea know there is no death, only change; there is no loss, only difficult gifts.

Even in the presence of profound loss there can be celebration. Joy is a choice.

JLH   Personal ritual is just that—personal. All that matters is that your personal rituals are meaningful to you. Whatever you do, do it with reverence. A prayer of thanks to the Creator—or just a prayer of thanks. A moment of silence. A moment merging in unity with all there is. A bowl of food lifted upward on fingertips with a whispered, "Thanks for everything." A glass of wine toasting the sunset. A candle. Incense. Sage. A small altar topped with special objects. An intentional practice of Qigong or yoga. A sunset walk on the beach.

The following is a Qigong practice called Release. It lifts the weight of the world from my shoulders. Try it—see if it has great power for you.

TODAY IN MY WORLD:

Choose a quiet place, and stand comfortably with feet parallel to each other, shoulder-width apart. Bend your knees slightly, and touch the tip of your tongue to the roof of your mouth. Hold your arms out in front of you with your elbows bent and your palms parallel to each other—about six inches apart. Focus your mind on your breathing.

Take a deep breath, and exhale with a resonant *mmmm* sound. Bend slightly at the waist and reach down with both hands—with palms still about six inches apart. Choose something that is very important to you and that you don't think you could stand to lose—such as your house, your favorite sport, your pet, your relationship with a loved one, your hearing, your eyesight, your life. Visualize holding your important something between your hands.

Rise slowly and bring your hands—still six inches apart, and still holding your treasure—to your heart. Feel intense love and gratitude for every joyful instant that you have spent with your important something. Now slowly raise your hands above your head, spread your hands apart, and *release* your treasure back to the Universe. It never belonged to you anyway—it was just on short-term loan from Spirit.

Chose another important something and release it. For everything important in your life, pick it up, love it, nurture it, give thanks for it, and then release it.

Do the same exercise for each person you have ever loved and has passed from this life. Hold them, love them, give thanks for them, and then release them back to the Universe.

Now, release your burdens—your fears, regrets, guilts, shames, embarrassments, angers. One by one, pick up each memory or fear that troubles you, hold it close, and release it to the Universe. Release each incident from your past that still bothers you. Release each fear—your fears about your health, your family, your job, and every other fear.

PLAY AND WHIMSEY

MAR My friend Tate must have been five at the time. Ever since she came to the planet, she's been a remarkable reminder of perspective. One day, a station wagon went speeding past where we were standing, and the entire back area of the cargo area was filled to capacity with balloons. All colors, with all kinds of festively colored ribbons holding them loosely in place. Very loosely. She laughed and explained, "There goes a party on its way."

I laughed too. And I thought that day, and still do, that my friend is a party on her way. Even before Tate walked, she danced with her eyes. And the instant the soles of her feet held her upright, she started dancing about. And that girl's been dancing ever since. She dances for just about any reason. She dances a sad dance when she's feeling a little blue.

She dances in anticipation, in happiness, at possibility, with impatience. She dances when her favorite food's being prepared by her mom, whom I'm often told is the best cook in the world. Yes. She'll dance because she's lucky enough to have the best cook for a mother. I guess that makes that dance a dance of gratitude.

I can think of so many times that this young lady has invited me to dance. At my desk. When I was painting. Designing. Composing text. Invitations issued at inconvenient moments. Almost always I would decline the invitation at first. But this dancer has her ways of persuasion. She'd put on music that she knew to be my favorite and come back to me to offer the invitation again. There's always the strategy of persistence. Regardless of how that dancer got me out of my work chair, I was always glad once I was up and moving. A very innovative choreographer, sometimes she'd give me direction and other times we would just wing it and let the music determine our flashy moves.

Somebody could suggest that Tate's a dancer because her mother's quite a dancer. I think that might have something to do with it. More than that, Tate was born with a foot that got turned a bit the wrong way. And I think that every cell in her being naturally wants to be able to celebrate her perseverance, her healing, her ability to overcome. Dancing is as natural to my friend as writing is to me. In some ways I've thought they are much the same thing. She tells stories by moving her being; I tell stories by moving a pen. And both activities are a celebration.

I can think of a few times when Tate didn't have to badger me into dancing. Times when I had the music started when my friend arrived and I welcomed her on the tips of my toes, shoes kicked off, ready to rock and roll! I smile just thinking about our swirls and leaps and glorious gestures.

Life taps us much the same way as my young friend. A particular moment has a dance for its own reason. And the invitation is issued—sometimes at inconvenient times. Life isn't always as persistent as my friend. Occasionally we are only given one invitation to dance. Take it or not. It won't come again the same way.

With one eye on your priorities, keep the other eye open to these rare overtures. Jonathan loves to say, "Dance lightly with life." Even accepting one whimsical opportunity, stepping away from our perceptions of what must be done in a moment—every once in awhile—becomes a celebration in itself. These are the moments which become the stories we tell and the memories we treasure. I cannot tell you exactly what I was trying to paint when I finally succumbed to the earnest request to come dance with my friend and my sweet Labrador retriever. But I can describe in detail the scarves we used and how fun it was to run dog circles, dancing with Judah. How delightful it was to have Judah's paws on my shoulders and have Tate directing the next sequence of our steps. And how much fun it was to watch her tap Judah on his big dog shoulders and ask, "Cut in?"

Dancing lightly with life, being open to the generous invitations to joy that life slips in while we are busy doing something else, is the sweet stuff. The really really good part of our story. Read it, word for word. Don't speed past it.

Chapter 10
UNITY—With All Creation

AFFIRMATION I Am One With Spirit and All Creation—
I give thanks for the unity of all creation and for
everything that has brought me to this moment. I release
my entire being to the gentle nurture of Spirit. ॐ

*Out beyond ideas of wrongdoing and rightdoing,
there is a field. I will meet you there.*
—Rumi

*As we light a path for others, we naturally light our
own way.*
—mar

*When the vast cathedral of our being becomes a
sanctuary for all creation, we become the face of God.*
—jlh

JLH *Unity* is indefinable. People have sensed it from before history, but no one has ever given a description that would be useful to someone who has not experienced it. "Harmonious oneness" feels right to those who have experienced it, but is not helpful to those who have not.

> *I am one with the earth, with the water, with the fire, with all living things, with the air—with the air that I breathe, and we are all one with Spirit.*
> —jlh

Consistently experiencing unconditional unity with Spirit and all creation is something we can never achieve—even though Oneness is our natural state. The best we can do is to taste it for a moment—as when we are captivated by the wonder of a newborn baby emerging into the world. Generally, the more we desire unity, the less likely we are to experience it, because desire of any kind is an impediment to unity.

Across time and across cultures, the wise ones speak of the unity of everyone and everything. *Mitakuye Oyasin* ("All My Relations" or "We Are All Related") is a Lakota prayer on behalf of everyone and everything. It is a prayer of oneness and harmony with all forms of life: people on earth, ancestors in the spirit world, animals, trees and plants, the sun, water, the winds, and the earth. It reminds us of the unity innate in the Universe.

Namasté is a greeting of unity and acceptance that recognizes the equality of all and pays honor to the sacredness of interconnection. The sense of Namasté is: "The God in me greets the God in you. I bow to the divine within you." While saying Namasté, press the palms of the hands together in front of the heart and bow the head slightly.

We move closer to unity as we remove the obstacles that separate us from Spirit and from each other: perceived needs, wants, jealousies, possessiveness, greed, guilt, shame, ego. That is *not* to say that asceticism (self-denial) is a path to unity—asceticism is a perverse but strong expression of ego. As an example, consider money. While greed and hoarding are certainly impediments to unity, renouncing money and living in sack cloth is equally an impediment. That particular obstacle is removed only when one becomes completely indifferent to the presence or absence of money and material possessions—both one's own and that of others. The way to unity is through moderation, balance, the Middle Way.

THE VAST CATHEDRAL OF YOUR BEING

Welcome to the vast cathedral of your being. Its bishop's chair is your seat, for you are in charge of your own life. Its altar celebrates your unity with all creation. Its open doors are invitation to all of life. Its volume shelters the unlimited diversity of human thought and belief. Throughout your cathedral, incense and the songs of angels impart a sense of wonder and gratitude to the commonplace. The light of God illuminates the colored window on the eastern wall—a symbol of the promise of a new day.

Explore the vast cathedral of your being. Walk reverently down the center aisle. Skip playfully through the courtyard as you toss bread to the ducks in the reflection pond. Light a candle to honor your ancestors. Toss small gifts of surprise to the children in the gallery. Linger thoughtfully in the catacombs that house the treasures of timeless wisdom—the secrets of joyful living that are revealed anew to the seekers of each new generation.

Celebrate your heritage and tradition as you stand at your cathedral's altar in honor of ancient ritual. Lift your cup and merge with Spirit in celebration of unity with all those who came before.

Celebrate diversity as you welcome all creation into your cathedral home. Welcome yourself, welcome your family, welcome your friends, welcome your community, welcome those from foreign lands, welcome those with unfamiliar ideas and beliefs, welcome those who love you, welcome those who hate you, welcome those who do not understand your ways, welcome the spirit of all those who came before you, and welcome the promise of those yet to come.

Welcome your entire congregation as they enter your cathedral's loving embrace. Know unity with each—with their sorrows, their joys, their hopes, their loves, their angers, their resentments, their forgivenesses, their gratitudes. Discover your compassion in the candles lit for each soul that ever has or ever will touch your life.

Timeless Wisdoms

From before the dawn of history, timeless wisdoms have guided humanity in rediscovering our unbreakable, but often imperceptible, connection with Spirit. For over three thousand years, the great masters of each generation have discovered and rediscovered this same wisdom of the ages. These same secrets to accessing our connection with Spirit and achieving inner peace have been written in many languages and many styles since before the time of Moses, Lao Tzu, and the Buddha.

Have Patience!

Although compassion, unity, and connection to Spirit were well-known to the masters millennia ago, one would never guess it from today's news headlines.

Fear, anger, and violence are humanity's genetic inheritance. Our distant ancestors' survival depended upon them. Even though it often appears that those genetics are still dominating, be assured that there is nothing wrong with our world. Have patience. We are making amazing progress toward evolved consciousness.

If we visualize the time humans have existed as a twenty-four-hour day, civilization represents the last one minute—that is, it began at 11:59 P.M. If life—the origin of our genes—is imagined as the twenty-four-hour day, civilization represents only the last one tenth of a second.

The prevalence of paranoid xenophobia and preemptive aggression in the world today should not surprise us. The true surprise is that so many of us have evolved so rapidly during this most recent one minute of humanity's day.

Have patience. Look at how far we have come just over the last few hundred years. Slavery has been abolished in most of the world. Murder within one's home community is no longer acceptable—except in the form of capital punishment in some places. If that statement provokes a "Ho-hum, that's nothing new" reaction, consider that in 1804 the sitting vice president of the United States, Aaron Burr, killed the former Secretary of the Treasury Alexander Hamilton (the guy on the $10 bill) in a legal duel.

Yes, patience. It is amazing that any countries have any form of democracy. It is amazing that any countries provide any degree of freedom of religion. We may think of the Pilgrims arriving at Plymouth Rock as escaping persecution and seeking freedom, but in reality, anyone who spoke a single word against the established religion in the Plymouth colony was subject to imprisonment, flogging, or worse. That was only four hundred years ago—that's eleven seconds on our twenty-four-hour clock of human existence.

Patience! It is amazing that *any* of us chooses unconditional love, universal peace, and compassion for all. Why should we expect that the paranoid xenophobia that humans have evolved over three million years should be reversed in a single generation? Just wait—maybe a thousand years, maybe only a few hundred—it's only a few seconds on the clock of humanity's existence, and not even the blink of an eye to Spirit.

Today, while we focus on radiating our unconditional love into the world and working toward world peace, let us also have compassion for the residual effects of humanity's highly evolved survival mechanisms.

Let us choose not to frustrate ourselves with the futile expectation that those around us should be more evolved, but rather, to bless all humans with our understanding and with our intention for an inspired and inspiring future.

PEACE IS THE ULTIMATE BLESSING

Peace is the ultimate blessing.

—Jewish traditional

I am one with Spirit. Spirit is within me. Spirit permeates me and surrounds me. Spirit is my comfort and my strength. I am one with Spirit.

—jlh

Peace wears many faces, but in the end, peace begins with me.

The humanitarian Mother Teresa said that she would not march against war, but would be happy to march for peace. As she recognized, peace can never be achieved through violence or anger. The only path to peace is compassion. The next part of the recipe for peace is one with which Mother Teresa would perhaps not have agreed: True compassion is only possible in the absence of fixed beliefs.

COMPASSION: UNCONDITIONAL LOVE AND ACCEPTANCE

Compassion, the desire to alleviate another's suffering, is best visualized by imagining the feelings of a loving mother toward her small child, and then extending those feelings toward every human—perhaps toward every living being.

Although not all mothers live up to the ideal, we associate mother love with loving one's children regardless of their actions— spilled milk, broken figurine, baseball through the window.

Compassion blooms where there is no expectation.
—jlh

Universal compassion extends that mother love to all actions by all people. True compassion is what enables us to love all people unconditionally and to accept all their actions without expectation or disappointment.

Can I have true compassion toward some people and not toward others? Only you can answer that. In this book, we use *compassion* as shorthand for "universal compassion"—the desire to alleviate suffering in the world, the suffering of all people.

TODAY IN MY WORLD:

Contemplate . . . Can you stretch to have compassion for all people, at all times, under all circumstances, and regardless of what those people do or don't do? Truly universal compassion would include compassion for the murderer. Can you do that? Do you choose to do that?

Does compassion extend to our dealings with animals? Where do we draw the line? Jains consider it unacceptable even to kill an insect. Most people don't go that far. Is it OK to squash a bug?

Kill a mouse? A cow? A cat or dog? A dolphin or whale? A chimpanzee? An Arab? The guy down the street with the funny look? Personally, while I honor the Jains' reverence for all life, I confess not only to squashing bugs, but to spraying them with chemical weapons of mass destruction. I'm also partial to hamburgers—knowing full well how they reached my table. What does that say about me? There's room for many points of view.

Unless your reverence for all beings extends to avoiding flyswatters and antibiotics, your "unconditional" compassion toward all life is conditional. This is certainly not a criticism—just an observation. We are all human, and human values are never absolute. Let us be compassionate toward ourselves as well as to all humans and to as many animals as our natures allow us to encompass. Generosity is a close relative of compassion, but lacks compassion's unique quality of being unlimited. A little compassion is good, and more is better. There is no such thing as too much compassion as far as I can see. Generosity, however, like virtually every other generally positive quality, becomes a curse in excess.

Generosity—I'm Happier when I Serve

Know first that you have absolutely no power to change the world, and then address all your energies and intent toward improving it.

—jlh

Others benefit directly when we are of service—that should require no further explanation. What is much less obvious is the benefit that accrues to ourselves when we serve others. We could discuss the biochemistry, the psychology, the theology, and the evolutionary survival value of cooperation, but the bottom line is that we feel good when we are of service—up to a point. If you haven't generally been inclined to serve, give it a try—whether publicly or with family and friends. Too much of *any* good thing isn't great, however, and soon we will address meddling and rescuing and how they differ from service.

MAR My life mission statement contains an element which seems contradictory. I assert I want anonymous generosity and public citizenship. This is my leaning toward unity and community. Citizenship is an invitation to participate in an agreed-upon process. Voting. Referendums. Debate. Elections. Expressing opinions to our elected officials. Volunteering toward positive social and political change. These are public demonstrations of my citizenship. They are part of my sense of community.

Anonymous generosity is a component of my sense of unity. Most of the time, I identify myself when I gift a friend for a birthday, Hanukkah, and such. My personal preference for other types of giving is to remain anonymous. The perception of someone being less fortunate than me has always made me uncomfortable in that it feels like a judgment I am assessing on another soul. My personal sense of compassion shines more brightly when my generosity is extended in the dark. When I gave corporately, for example, I considered it a part of my marketing plan. Because when individuals observe a company giving, it is good for that company's perception within its community. When I give anonymously, personally, I have a sense of moving toward unity. I feel part of a greater goodness.

There are distinctions between giving and grandstanding. Such thin lines are drawn between compassionate assistance and functional meddling.

Meddling and Rescuing—Shadows of Compassion

My ego drives me into your business.

—jlh

JLH Byron Katie speaks of "three kinds of business in the universe: mine, yours, and God's." Everything that happens in the world, or doesn't happen in the world, is *not* my responsibility. There are more than enough things that *are* my responsibility. I am responsible for my thoughts, my beliefs, and my actions— and that is enough. It does not serve me to mind your business. I can only make myself unhappy by trying to second-guess what anyone else thinks or does.

Great—that's easy enough to say in the abstract, but when the other person is our country's president, or is our spouse, parent, child, or boss, it doesn't come naturally at all to remain detached. For many of us, staying in our own business requires a lifetime of self-reminders.

Unsolicited advice is always meddling.

—jlh

Often we meddle out of a sincere desire to help another, so how can we know when have we gone too far? We have overstepped our bounds whenever we cross the line from assisting others to get what *they want* to believing that we know better than they what they *should* want.

Rescuing is repeatedly coming to the aid of someone in a way that does not honor that person. If we do not fully respect the person we are assisting, it is likely that we are rescuing. There is an old proverb about teaching a man to fish versus giving him another fish each day. That proverb is about rescuing. Teaching someone to fish enables them to prosper with honor. Doling out fish after fish—probably with a growing feeling of being burdened—is rescuing. If you are considering aiding a family member or friend, do it in a way that enhances their honor—or don't do it.

MAR Bill Clinton frequently models a process for evaluating unity, benefit for the greater good. He asks, "Are we better off, in whole, today, than we were when we started this thing?" Whatever that thing may be, we can apply this statement.

TODAY IN MY WORLD:

As you go through your day today, and especially as you observe your friends and family interact, observe whenever you feel compelled to make someone else's business your business. Ask yourself whether whatever action you are considering honors that person and supports what he or she wants.

Honor everyone's uniqueness. When we have expectations, we believe that we know how people should behave, and we can have no compassion. Once we accept that the "right" path is unique to each of us, we can be compassionate.

TOUCHING THE INFINITE

I do not have to agree with or understand all the sacred texts of the world to benefit from them. Sacred texts are humanity's effort at tethering the infinite to the finite. I choose to take value from the presence of that tether, to take lesson and to observe some fundamental principles. One of my lifelong habits in reading sacred texts is to repeatedly read the text in many different versions, do some word study in translations from the original language, and then, with my own understanding, paraphrase the text for my own use.

Here is one of my favorites resulting from that method of study and observation: taken from the New Testament of the Bible . . . Romans 12: 9-21:

> Demonstrate your adoration of God in these ways:
>
> Let your love be true. Put away harm and embrace good. Be as family to each other, prefer each other's company. Be thorough and productive, passionate in your spirit, grateful for promise, tolerant in challenge, constant in the practice of prayer, generous with your possessions. Open your home. Speak well of your enemies. Bring no harm with your word. Have deep empathy. Set down your arrogance. Walk easily in the company of all. Be balanced in dispensing justice: Allow God the right place for retribution. Do not be overwhelmed by unfairness, but rather govern your days with goodness.

Opening to Spirit

Spirit is always waiting to rush into us, but we are too full of worldly things. It is like trying to pour fine wine into a cup filled with mud—the wine is waiting, but the mud must be removed first.

—jlh

JLH Each tradition has its own ways of touching Spirit—from the Christian sharing of bread and wine to the Sufi whirling dance. Some ways of touching Spirit have developed a life of their own apart from the tradition they sprang from. What we refer to simply as yoga and is as widely available as aerobics classes in many cities is more precisely Hatha Yoga and, like all forms of yoga, is a derivative of spiritual practices of ancient India. Qigong originated as a Taoist practice in China, but like yoga, is now accessible to all.

TODAY IN MY WORLD:
THE INNER SMILE:

The Inner Smile is a Qigong exercise that quiets the mind and creates a profound sense of inner peace.

While Qigong is in general a moving meditation like its off-spring tai chi, this is one of the few Qigong exercises that does not include physical movement, and it is also one of the simplest and most powerful.

Choose a chair with firm support, and sit comfortably in a quiet place, with feet flat on the floor. Let your hands rest on your thighs with your palms up. Lift the corners of your mouth very slightly into just the beginning of a smile. Close your eyes, or better yet, half close them. Take a very deep breath and slowly release the breath completely, with mouth closed, while making a quiet *mmmm* sound. Feel the *mmmm* vibrate your mouth and head. To help with the smile and the *mmmm* sound, visualize being very content—like after a Thanksgiving dinner, or after great sex, or after a fun but tiring day at the beach. Repeat the deep inhale and the slow exhale with the quiet *mmmm*. Let whatever you visualized to start the contentment fade to gray, and focus your entire attention on the slight smile, your breathing, and the *mmmm* sound. Continue for at least three minutes.

Aum is the most primordial human sound—and the sound most connected to Spirit. *Aum* is pronounced in three parts: 1) ă, 2) o͞o (as in boot), 3) m. When you pronounce *aum*, the *a*—a throat sound that vibrates in the abdomen—signifies waking.

The *u*—a tongue sound that vibrates in the chest—signifies dreaming. The *m*—a lip sound that vibrates in the head—signifies sleeping.

Now, substitute the three-part *aum* sound for the *mmmm* sound. While your mouth will lose the smile shape during the first two of the three sounds in *aum,* concentrate on reforming the slight smile during the *m* part of each *aum.*

You don't need to be sitting to do the Inner Smile exercise. You can do a variation of the Inner Smile while walking, while lying down (it works much better than counting sheep, as a sleep aid), or any other time when thinking and attention are not required.

Caution: Do *not* do the Inner Smile exercise (or any other form of meditation) while driving.

Once you are able to sustain a state of relaxation and contentment, with your mind remaining blank, you are ready to try a more advanced form of the exercise. Visualize your face smiling, without actually lifting the corners of your mouth, and visualize the deep exhale with *mmmm* sound, while remaining silent.

Tomorrow, take an early morning walk in silence while maintaining an inner smile. Better yet, do it every day for the next fifty years.

Afterword

JLH Ending (and beginning) our days and our projects with a personal prayer gives focus and completion, as well as thanksgiving. This is my own personal prayer—the connection with Spirit that I have found throughout the great wisdoms of the ages, and set in the phrasing of my Christian youth.

> Lord God, Holy Spirit, giver of all light, bless and keep all those of this world. Grant us your peace, your light, your love. Grant us complete renewal of body, mind, and spirit— continual rebirth in newness of life. Let your light shine upon us and be gracious to us.
>
> Grant to each and every one of us: health, comfort, joy, peace within ourselves, peace within our families, peace within our communities, and peace among all those of this world.
>
> Grant that I may be an instrument of thy peace. Grant that I may radiate thy peace, thy light, thy love, thy healing, thy comfort, thy joy, to all those around me and all those in my thoughts this day and ever more. Amen.

There is great power in the daily repetition of a prayer that uniquely expresses your relationship with Spirit—whatever Spirit means to you. I strongly encourage you to develop your own personal prayer. If you like, take inspiration from the prayers of your religious community, but make the prayer you create truly your own. A successful personal prayer conveys a clear message, generates a profound image, and reaffirms your heartfelt convictions.

LET US WISH YOU ON YOUR WAY

Simply an Inspired Life—SAILing

It is now time to go into the world and live Simply an Inspired Life—to go SAILing, as it were. Your broader perspectives now provide release from emotional pain. You can discern the difference between a story rooted in self-inflicted suffering and one springing from joy.

Your opportunity is always to make the choice for joy, to see the world with new eyes, open eyes, loving eyes. To choose compassion and understanding—for yourself, your family, your friends, your community, for the whole world.

Your opportunity is to soar your Spirit. See light and joy in everything. Spread your wings and fly boldly. Give thanks for rainbows and butterflies—symbols of renewal and rebirth. Offer daily thanksgiving—for yourself, your family, your friends, your community, for the whole world.

Your opportunity is to visualize a kinder world. To sing glad songs of tomorrow—imagining a world of love—of the whole world filled with love. To offer your hand . . . often. To breathe deeply and honor yourself. To pause and contemplate your gratitude—for *all* of life.

Honor your past. Choose to tell joyful stories of your history. Live an observed life, always being conscious of the attitudes you hold. Continue to train yourself to observe life from new perspectives that support an ever higher quality of living. Always monitor your priorities. Chart your course. Set SAIL with courage.

MAR Yes. Set SAIL with courageous Action. SAIL with the companions of Honor, Forgiveness, Gratitude, Choice, Vision, Celebration, and Unity. Continue writing this book with the processes and exercises unique to your way of seeing. Jonathan loves to say, "Today is your day to dance lightly with life."

As you choose your profound, passionate, and inspired life, may there be *unity* above you, drawing your sights higher;

May there be *honor* below you, rooting you in your grace and goodness;

May you sense *vision* ever before you, inspiring you daily into your dreams;

May there be *action* behind you, boldly supporting your choices;

And may your knowledge of the connection to *choice* strengthen you;

May *gratitude* be the fire in your belly, invigorating and enlivening you;

May *celebration* be the soundtrack of all your journeys;

And may *forgiveness* be the light for every step you take.

May you embrace every moment and in each moment have the wisdom to choose joy.

It's easy to succumb to the idea that we're waiting for more ideal circumstances for the dreams we've held to begin. Waiting for that idealized someday . . .

Everyone waits . . . longs for . . . everyone has a someday . . .

Some people wake up and discover that the calendar in real time reads nothing but now.

Now is *your* time to *live*.

Make the choices to live Simply an Inspired Life.

Acknowledgments

MARY ANNE:

Conari for vision. Jan Johnson, publisher, who held the acronym of SAIL with an open palm and shared it. The whole team at Conari who are not listed by name—but who see their name written in the collective quality of our offering. Hugh Prather for presenting a viable road to a young woman. My friend, Jonathan, for the bold courage demonstrated by becoming my coauthor. Your dedication, flexibility, and willingness to ride the many storms of a writer's life have been a marvel. My husband, David, who has understood, and listened with such an informed heart. Suze, who hangs out with the blue herons, has gently let this project take its own course. Readers Barbara, Caren, Ellen, and Paula . . . your time and trusted commentary improved this message. And the choir members who sing from my history—thank you for the lessons. And your generosity of spirit to allow some of our shared stories on these pages.

JONATHAN:

Mary Anne, thank you for suggesting that we coauthor, for your steadfast and loving commitment to our partnership, and for gracefully weathering the challenges of integrating our sometimes divergent approaches to this project. My wife, Suze, thank you for adapting gracefully and lovingly to my extensive and erratic writing hours, and for making my life easy and joyful in all ways. The extraordinary team at Conari, thank you for your support, your enthusiasm, and your skill.

Resources

Our website, *www.SimplyanInspiredLife.com,* provides an ongoing community for those who wish to make the principles of Simply an Inspired Life a continuing part of their lives.

The site offers the opportunity to:

- Sign up for free Daily Inspiration e-mail and newsletters.
- Join the discussion group to support and receive support from others committed to SAILing as a way of life.
- Learn of workshops, online classes, one-on-one coaching, and appearances by the authors.
- Locate recommended books and other resources for following up on ideas suggested in this book—books by great teachers, transformative programs, residential retreat centers, Qigong teachers and videos, and more.

Our other websites are:

Mary Anne: *www.MaryAnneRadmacher.net*
Jonathan: *www.JonathanLockwoodHuie.com*

About the Authors

Mary Anne Radmacher is an acclaimed author and artist whose work has been featured on CNN, HGTV, Oprah, and in *The New Yorker*. She is the creator of *Courage Doesn't Always Roar* and *May Your Walls Know Joy,* the author of *Lean Forward into Your Life* and *Live Boldly,* and creator of beautiful calendars by the same name. She has been a writer, artist, and entrepreneur for more than a quarter of a century. She lives with her husband on Whidbey Island, Washington. Visit her at *www.maryanneradmacher.net.*

Jonathan Lockwood Huie is well into his next act. Following a successful career in the go-go world of high-tech start ups, Jonathan deepened his search for meaning, wisdom, and peace. Huie has a mission to teach self-awareness through his writing, his seminars, and his website. He and his wife live in St. Petersburg, Florida and on Whidbey Island. Visit him at *www.jonathanlockwoodhuie.com.*

Also visit the *Simply an Inspired Life* website,
www.SimplyanInspiredLife.com.

To Our Readers

Conari Press, an imprint of Red Wheel/Weiser, publishes books on topics ranging from spirituality, personal growth, and relationships to women's issues, parenting, and social issues. Our mission is to publish quality books that will make a difference in people's lives—how we feel about ourselves and how we relate to one another. We value integrity, compassion, and receptivity, both in the books we publish and in the way we do business.

Our readers are our most important resource, and we value your input, suggestions, and ideas about what you would like to see published. Please feel free to contact us, to request our latest book catalog, or to be added to our mailing list.

Conari Press
An imprint of Red Wheel/Weiser, LLC
500 Third Street, Suite 230
San Francisco, CA 94107
www.redwheelweiser.com